This book examines how companies cope with the pressures which are unleashed by recessions. It is based on a large-scale survey undertaken in the Spring of 1993 which elicited the participation of more than 600 leading UK companies. The questionnaire data were combined with a long time series of data on the financial performance of most of the companies so that it was possible to trace effects left over from the recession in the early 1980s. The four main issues examined in the book are as follows. What makes companies vulnerable to recessionary pressures? How do companies typically respond to these pressures? How have recessionary pressures been transmitted back into labour markets, and what kinds of institutional changes have they induced? Finally, do recessionary pressures stimulate innovative activity?

THE NATIONAL INSTITUTE OF
ECONOMIC AND SOCIAL RESEARCH

Economic and Social Studies

XXXVIII

COPING WITH RECESSION: UK COMPANY
PERFORMANCE IN ADVERSITY

COPING WITH RECESSION
UK Company performance in adversity

by

P. A. GEROSKI

and

P. GREGG

CAMBRIDGE
UNIVERSITY PRESS

CAMBRIDGE
UNIVERSITY PRESS

University Printing House, Cambridge CB2 8BS, United Kingdom

Cambridge University Press is part of the University of Cambridge.

It furthers the University's mission by disseminating knowledge in the pursuit of
education, learning and research at the highest international levels of excellence.

www.cambridge.org
Information on this title: www.cambridge.org/9780521622769

© The National Institute of Economic and Social Research 1997

First published 1997

A catalogue record for this publication is available from the British Library

ISBN 978-0-521-62276-9 Hardback
ISBN 978-0-521-62601-9 Paperback

We would like to dedicate this book to our families, not least because of their wisdom in steering clear of this project and just letting us get on with it. They missed some fun and a few interesting puzzles, but coped admirably with these and other deprivations.

Contents

x   Coping with recession

Figures and tables

Tables   *page*

ACKNOWLEDGEMENTS

We would like to thank the Gatsby Foundation for financing this project, and our host institutions, the Centre for Business Strategy at London Business School, the National Institute of Economic and Social Research and Australian National University, for all other forms of support. John O'Sullivan and Garry Young helped with some of the aggregate data, while Thibault Desjonqueres and Arnaud Langlois helped dispatch the questionnaire, tabulate the results and analyse the data, proving themselves to be indispensable collaborators in the process. We received positive feedback from a wide variety of sources in the three years it took us to write this book. Editors and referees from the *National Institute Economic Review*, the *Business Strategy Review*, the *British Journal of Industrial Relations*, *New Economy* and the *European Economic Review* provided helpful comments on parts of this work, as did seminar audiences at London Guildhall University, the University of Auckland, the Australian National University, the University of Tasmania, La Trobe University and the London Business School. Andrew Britton was an early sounding board for this project, and provided encouragement and support throughout. Martin Weale, Jonathan Haskell, and Kimya Kamshad provided helpful comments on an earlier draft of the manuscript, stimulating a number of important revisions. Last but by no means least, we are very grateful to Christine VanderNoot for putting the whole thing together with her usual good humour and efficiency. Needless to say, the usual disclaimer applies.

1   Introduction

Recessions as natural experiments

Economics is, by and large, a non-experimental science, something which makes applied research in economics both very interesting and very challenging. Scholars who are, for example, interested in observing how companies respond to competitive pressure cannot simply dump a firm into a test tube and turn up the bunsen burner. Similarly, very few managers will allow a scientist to dissect their organisation or induce a major crisis in one of its operations just to see if what happens is consistent with some hypothesis derived from economic theory. What this means is that, on the whole, few theories or hypotheses in economics can be directly tested (or compared with alternatives) using controlled experiments.

Many economists have tried to overcome this problem by using data generated from the ordinary day-to-day activities of firms, as if the market were continually conducting experiments on its own and making the data publicly available. For example, scholars interested in understanding what it is that makes some firms outperform others often make simple comparisons between firms, isolating differences in some aspect of a company's strategy, structure or market circumstances and then trying to associate it with differences in performance. Needless to say, the value of such comparisons depends on how carefully extraneous disturbances have been controlled for, and on how accurately various experimental causes or effects have been measured. More importantly, such comparisons are useful only if the sample displays enough variation to cover the entire range of circumstances which firms typically find themselves in. If, for example, the data describes similar firms operating in similar circumstances that happen to prevail at some particular time, then even the most sophisticated analysis of the sample will not yield much useful information about the performance of other firms in other circumstances at different times. That

1

is, the value of 'experimental' data thrown up by the market depends on whether the market conducts interesting experiments on a routine basis. This seems unlikely. Many markets have long stretches of 'normal' activity punctuated by major changes as new market segments or production technologies arise and expand, and old niches or organisational routines decline. The day-to-day life of many firms seems to have the same irregular pattern: spells of routine activity punctuated by the odd crisis. In these circumstances, routinely generated market data contains only a relatively limited amount of useful information about what happens to firms during crises. An alternative and, on the face of it, more promising methodology is to try and find some kind of unusual market event which resembles the laboratory experiment one would like to conduct (that is, induces a crisis similar to those one wants to examine), and then analyse the circumstances surrounding that natural event as if it had occurred in a laboratory. As long as such 'natural experiments' have causes which are unrelated to the particular issues being studied, they should yield unusually valuable information.[1] Those scholars interested in the determinants of company performance, for example, might wish to conduct an experiment which subjects a firm to sudden, unexpected and very extreme pressure for a sustained period of time, say by moving its demand curve sharply inward. Amongst the experimental effects which one might focus on are: whether the firm lowers its price (and if so by how much), whether it tries to reduce its costs, how much of the shock it passes on to various stakeholders (like shareholders or workers), whether it exits from the market, and so on. The analogous 'natural experiment' would be to observe the activities of a firm whose market contracts suddenly and severely, as might happen in a cyclical downturn.

Indeed, in many ways recessions are an interesting 'natural experiment' to monitor: they involve a major contraction in demand sustained over a substantial period of time, they affect some firms far more than others and they are exogenous to the actions of individual firms (although not necessarily to the actions of all firms taken together). That the contraction in demand is major and sustained means that those firms who are badly affected by a recession are likely to be forced to rethink the fundamental premises of their competitive strategy, and cannot simply initiate holding actions to wait out the storm. The comparison between the strategy and structure of firms who are extremely severely affected by a recession with those of firms less severely affected provides evidence on what makes some firms more vulnerable to shocks than others, and on the robustness of different strategy choices and different organisational structures to changes in market circumstances. Although the fact that an event is exogenous does not mean that its occurrence is a surprise, many firms do not, in fact, anticipate the depth or duration of recessions. As a consequence, recessions also throw at least some useful light on how firms respond to unexpected changes in demand. Further, the effects of recessionary demand shocks are inevitably transferred back to labour markets (as well as to suppliers of capital equipment and other inputs), and taking a microeconomic view of the process may help to illuminate the mechanism by which shocks are transmitted between output markets and the input markets which supply them, and the effects they induce when they arrive. Finally, the fact that recessions are exogenous to the actions of individual firms makes the experimental setting relatively clean and complete: from the point of view of an affected firm, the 'experiment' starts when the exogenous event occurs and ends when all of its effects have been realised.

The next best thing to inducing a recession for research purposes is to take advantage of a recession which occurs for other reasons. We have chosen to use the Major–Lamont recession which began in the middle of 1990 as a 'natural experiment' to use in studying company performance. Our goal is to use data thrown up by that recession to examine how firms react to extreme adversity, and our hope is that such an examination will yield some insights into the mechanisms through which firms both initiate and then manage change in the face of extreme adversity.

The Major–Lamont recession

The macroeconomic performance of the UK economy over recent decades is a depressingly familiar story of underachievement and macroeconomic mismanagement. The golden age of the postwar period (it was less golden in the UK than elsewhere) ended in the early 1970s. Although the oil price shock of 1973 and the associated slump in GDP growth that followed are often used to date this transition, oil (and other commodity) price rises were only one of several factors which caused the stagflation of the 1970s (others included acrimonious labour relations and the cumulative effects of underinvestment in training, R&D and basic infrastructure). The apparent malaise of the period and general disenchantment with conventional methods of demand management helped pave the way for Mrs Thatcher's supply-side revolution and associated monetarist policies. The 'return to sound money' policy she initiated in 1979 led almost immediately to a major recession in the early 1980s and was, in turn, followed by a consumer led boom generated in the run up to the 1987 election. The fragility of that boom and a possibly inappropriate pegging of sterling in

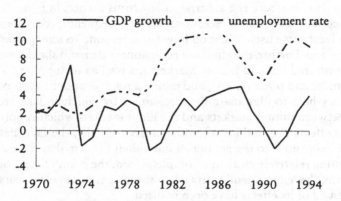

Figure 1.1 *Real GDP growth and the unemployment rate*

the ERM contributed to the creation of a second major recession in the early 1990s.[2]

Figure 1.1 shows the simplest and most familiar picture of the cyclical ups and downs which characterised the period using data on unemployment and real GDP growth. It is not a pretty picture.[3] Unemployment rose from about 2.1 per cent in 1970 to 9.4 per cent in 1994. This increase in unemployment was fairly irregular, jumping from 4.9 per cent in 1980 to 8.0 per cent in 1981 and from 5.7 per cent in 1990 to 7.8 per cent in 1991. Unemployment peaked at 11.1 per cent in 1986 and at the slightly lower level of 10.3 per cent in 1993, bottoming out between these peaks at 5.7 per cent in 1990. Two major recessions, in 1980/81 and 1990/91, stand out clearly in the data on unemployment, as does the apparent hysteresis of the series: throughout the 1980s and early 1990s, the UK did not to return anywhere near to the 2 per cent unemployment rates characteristic of the early 1970s (or to the political resolve not to tolerate unemployment rates higher than the 2–3 per cent which was also a feature of the 1970s). In what follows, we will concentrate on the two more recent recessions (which had large rises in unemployment associated with them), at least in part because it is hard to extend our company data sets back through the early 1970s.

Figure 1.1 also displays movements in another commonly used cyclical indicator, namely real GDP growth. Curiously, this series suggests that a third recession occurred during the period 1974–6, differentiated from the other two both by its rapid recovery as well as by the lack of an associated rise in unemployment. Like employment, GDP growth slumped in 1980 (falling 5 percentage points between 1979 and 1980) and again in 1990

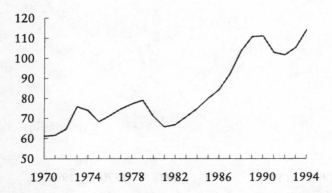

Figure 1.2 *Manufacturing output (£ billion, 1990 prices and 1990 weights)*

(falling by 2.4 percentage points). Average GDP growth over the 25 year period was 2.1 per cent (unemployment averaged 6.6 per cent), ranging from 7.4 per cent in 1973 to –2.2 per cent in 1980 (unemployment ranged from 2.1 per cent in 1970 to 11.1 per cent in 1986). Unlike unemployment, real GDP growth did not display any obvious signs of hysteresis over the period (high and low growth rates did not persist for long over time), although the recovery phase of both recessions was considerably longer than the preceding downturns were.

All of this adds up to a rather uneven macroeconomic performance. As Figure 1.2 shows, the only period of sustained growth in manufacturing output over the period 1970–94 occurred between 1982 and 1989 (manufacturing output grew by 29 per cent over these eight years), and this was sandwiched between recession induced falls in output of 6.2 per cent between 1980 and 1982 and 6 per cent between 1990 and 1992. Investment expenditures on plant and machinery fell by 6 per cent between 1980 and 1982 and by an astonishing 11 per cent between 1990 and 1992 (see Figure 1.3). Moreover, investment expenditures were relatively constant over the period 1970–80, and only began to rise sharply from 1984 or 1985. The increase in real investment expenditures from 1980 to 1990 was more than three times larger than that which occurred between 1970 and 1980. As Figure 1.4 shows, the consequence of high levels of investment in plant and high rates of growth of demand was higher productivity growth rates and, indeed, they were generally much higher in the 1980s than in the 1970s. This said, productivity growth fluctuated wildly throughout the 1980s, ranging from –5.9 per cent in 1980 to 7.2 per cent in 1983, and then

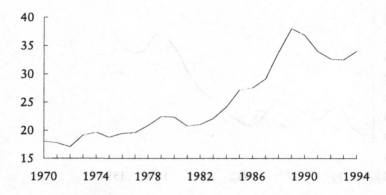

Figure 1.3 *Investment in plant and machinery (£ billion, 1990 prices)*

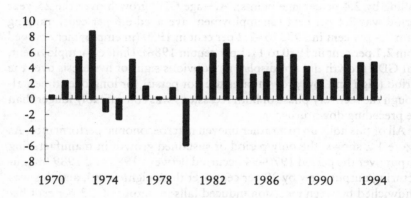

Figure 1.4 *Output per head in manufacturing (annual % change)*

falling to 3.2 per cent in 1985 before rising to 5.8 per cent in 1988. One of several causes of this volatility was movements in the level of economic activity over the cycle: the growth in output per head followed movements in real GDP growth fairly closely, displaying a clear pro-cyclical pattern of variation.

Procyclical variations in productivity ought to lead to countercyclical variations in unit costs, and Figure 1.5 shows that this was indeed the case. Unit costs are also driven by inflation, and the generally declining annual percentage increases in unit costs reflect the gradual reduction in inflation

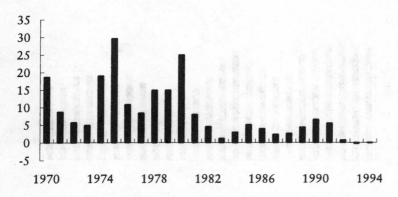

Figure 1.5 *Unit labour costs in manufacturing (annual % change)*

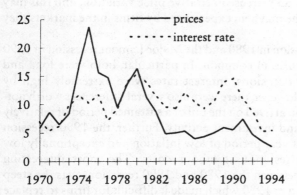

Figure 1.6 *Inflation and short-term interest rates (annual % change consumer expenditure deflator; 3-month Treasury bill)*

which was a main policy concern of the Thatcher government. Figure 1.6 shows movements in consumer prices over the period. Both the Thatcher and the Major-Lamont recessions were preceded by momentary rises in inflation, and, in both cases, interest rates also rose (to combat inflation and protect the exchange rate), increasing the financial pressure on firms who were already facing a decline in demand and a consequent rise in unit labour costs. Although this is not evident in the data shown on Figure 1.6, it seems likely that the two spurts of inflation in the early 1980s and 1990s

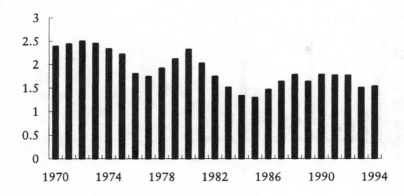

Figure 1.7 *Dollar exchange rate (US$/£)*

were accompanied by an increase in relative price variation, and this may have contributed to the mayhem experienced by firms in the markets they operated in.[4]

The Thatcher recession in 1980 and the Major-Lamont recession in 1990 had a number of features in common. In particular, both were long and severe and, on both occasions, interest rates were extremely high by historical standards. However, there were also several differences worth noting. The 1990 recession arrived on the tail of a sustained period of relatively high output growth and investment activity. Further, the 1990 recession followed a six to eight year period of low inflation and exceptionally low annual percentage rises in unit labour costs. The most interesting difference, however, between the 1980 and 1990 recessions was the steep appreciation of sterling in 1980 which made it difficult for firms to replace lost domestic orders with orders from abroad (see Figure 1.7). It is, perhaps, no coincidence that the recovery experienced in the mid-1980s was accompanied by a substantial devaluation in sterling. The 1990 recession, by contrast, occurred during a period of relatively stable nominal exchange rates which reached levels about 20 per cent lower than in 1980. One expects, therefore, that one potentially observable difference between the two recessions is that export oriented firms would have been much more adversely affected in 1980 than in the recession of 1990.

The work that follows is based on a survey of firms which we undertook in the spring of 1993. To help put the responses that we received into a broader macroeconomic context, it is useful to examine Figures 1.8–1.11 which show quarterly movements in GDP growth, unemployment, invest-

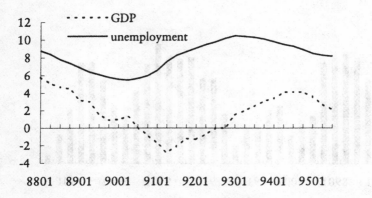

Figure 1.8 *Real GDP growth and the unemployment rate*

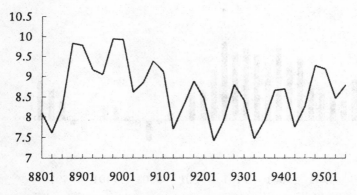

Figure 1.9 *Investment in plant and machinery[a] (quarterly, £ billion, 1990 prices)*
[a]*Defined as the sum of private sector, public corporation and general government investments.*

ment output per head and unit labour costs from 1988–95. Figure 1.8 shows that in the Spring of 1993, unemployment was peaking (it began to fall at a slow rate immediately thereafter). Although this suggests that the recession was far from over, the Spring of 1993 also saw the eighth quarter of successive increases in the rate of real GDP growth (and the second successive quarter in which the rate of growth of real GDP was positive). Similarly, Figure 1.9 shows that investment expenditures surged slightly at

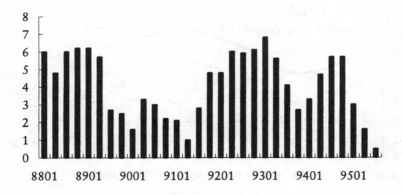

Figure 1.10 *Output per head in manufacturing (annual % change)*

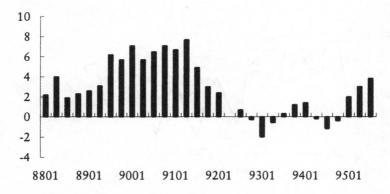

Figure 1.11 *Unit labour costs in manufacturing (annual % change)*

the end of 1992 (in what might have been a regular seasonal fluctuation), but showed no signs of secular rise (and had not regained its peak in early 1990). By the Spring of 1993, output per head had (like real GDP growth) been growing at erratically increasing rates for seven successive quarters (Figure 1.10), while unit labour costs had been falling for at least a year and increasing at declining rates for at least a year before that (Figure 1.11). All in all, one might have expected many firms to believe that the recession was all but over in the Spring of 1993, although this perception would not have been shared by many of those with jobs and virtually everyone who was unemployed.

The issues

Many people, economists and popular commentators alike, believe that recessions are periods of waste and stagnation. The sight of long (and lengthening) dole queues, derelict industrial sites and a large and growing list of failed firms makes it hard to believe that recessions are part of the natural functioning of the economy, or to accept that the havoc which they apparently wreak may serve any useful purpose. As a consequence, there is a great deal of support for the proposition that everyone can be made better off if the economy remains on an even keel.[5]

This view is, however, disputed by some who have argued that recessions are a time when major structural change occurs within markets and inside the firms which populate them. The idea is not dissimilar to those articulated by Schumpeter in his famous vision of 'gales of creative destruction'; that is, of waves of innovations which displace earlier innovations whose markets have become satiated and stagnated. These bursts of innovative activity are likely to have two important consequences: they propel the economy out of recession and, because they induce structural change in otherwise stagnant markets, they stimulate long-run growth.[6] More recent arguments of this type have focused on cyclical variations in the opportunity costs of change. Any organisation which plans to expand, contract or refocus its activities in some way needs to manage this change, and providing resources for managing change usually means withdrawing them from activities like producing and selling in some markets. Redirecting these resources will always be costly, but the costs of doing so will be lower when producing and selling is relatively unprofitable, provided they do not require large investment expenditures.[7] Since this is likely to be the case during a recession, one is likely to observe more organisational changes during a recession than a boom. This argument, sometimes referred to as the 'pit-stop' theory of recession, predicts that firms will make investments during recessions which intensively utilise factors of production (principally management and labour) whose opportunity costs are relatively low.[8]

The interesting difference between Schumpeterian visions of what happens during recessions and the pit-stop theory of recession is that the former describes a process of external, market driven change, while the latter is internal and strategy driven. In many Schumpeterian stories, new entry is the vehicle by which new innovations reach the market; the displacement of new products and processes by new ones occurs, in the main, as new firms drive out old firms. The pit-stop theory of the firm, on the other hand, describes a process by which established firms adapt their internal structures, making various types of investments using standard cost-benefit calculations that have been augmented (as they should be) by an explicit consideration of opportunity costs. In what follows, we will focus mainly on internal restructuring, a choice which is dictated by the nature of our data but consistent with our view that, slow as it can be, internal strategy driven change is often the major vehicle of change in established markets.[9]

Our data on the Major-Lamont recession is, in a sense, a single observation, and it is most useful to analyse the data in the spirit of doing a case study which tries to cast light on the mechanisms by which changes occur during particular recessions. Using a well designed case study, it is possible to develop a feel for when major structural changes occur over the trade cycle, and for the relative importance of internal and external driven change in recessions. What is more, micro based empirical work (case based or not) enables one to identify the important mechanisms of change: the *who?*, *what?* and *how?* of the process. Such data helps to provide answers to questions like: *which firms are most seriously affected by recessionary pressures; what types of decisions do they make in response to the pressures which they face;* and, *how do these responses affect their survival prospects and the well-being of the markets which they operate in?*.

Thus, our goal in what follows is to examine the effects of recessions from as microeconomic a viewpoint as is possible. Our discussion will focus on the four following issues: (i) selection pressures, (ii) the response to adversity; (iii) feedback to the labour market; and (iv) innovation.

Selection pressures

Economists believe that selection pressures weed out the less efficient firms from markets, creating room for more efficient and more able firms to enter, grow and prosper. The difficulty with selection pressures, however, is that they can be short-sighted whenever they use current performance to separate winners from losers and neglect to evaluate fully a firm's future prospects.[10] If fundamentally sound firms experience transitory difficulties (say arising from adjustment costs associated with rapid expansion) during unexpected economic downturns, then they may be selected against despite having good long-run prospects. Needless to say, this is likely to inflate the costs of recession induced industrial restructuring. Although we are not in a position to mount rigorously persuasive tests of the proposition that selection pressures accurately identify firms that are fundamentally unsound, we will try to generate at least some impressionistic evidence about whether firms that are fundamentally sound but suffer from transitory difficulties are selected against.

One of the most interesting features of recessions is the fact that some companies seem to be much more severely affected by recessionary pressures than others. Indeed, some firms actually prosper in bad times, particularly those sheltering in well protected niches of otherwise badly affected markets (liquidators also typically do well). Although there is little doubt that recessionary squeezes affect some sectors more severely than others, it is difficult to believe that selection pressures are wholly, or even mainly, sector specific. Even the most casual empiricism suggests that there is a substantial degree of heterogeneity in the effects of recessions on firms within particular sectors. This means that firm specific factors like size, strategy and organisational structure are likely to have a major effect on the vulnerability of firms to recessionary pressures. One of our goals in what follows is to identify the criteria which seem to select against some firms and in favour of others during economic downturns.

The response to adversity

Simple textbook descriptions of the effects of demand shocks usually confine attention to prices and quantities, pointing out that the relative size of price/quantity responses depends on the elasticity of the supply curve. In fact, firms have a wide range of strategic choices that they can make in the face of adversity. Many corporate strategy texts identify a small number of generic strategy choices which are typically open to firms, of which the two most important are *cost leadership* and *differentiation*. The idea behind the concept of generic strategies is that they identify mutually exclusive strategy choices and, in the current context, this makes them a natural organising device to use in focusing on the kinds of responses firms make to adversity.[11] Corporate strategy also encompasses financial management, and not a few people believe that many of the responses that firms make to recessionary pressures are no more than financial re-engineering. One of our goals in what follows is to try to identify whether firms typically focus on costs, differentiation or finance when they respond to recessionary pressures, and to isolate the particular strategic weapons they choose when they do respond.

One of the most characteristic features of recessions is that investment in plant and equipment falls off markedly as demand turns down. It is widely believed that financial pressures also force firms to slash a much wider range of investments in intangibles like market goodwill, training, and R&D. The problem with these arguments is that it is very

14 Coping with recession

difficult to be sure whether overheads are 'fat' or 'muscle', particularly when some support services have subtle and potentially very long-run effects on corporate performance. Although it is not possible to make much progress on the question of whether recessionary pressures cause firms to cut into muscle using our data, one can at least try to ascertain whether investments in different types of intangibles (such as R&D, new product or process innovation, training and marketing) are as adversely affected by recessionary pressures as investments in plant typically are. We will also try to identify the types of firms which bring forward different types of investments in the face of adverse demand shocks, and link this behaviour to the features of corporate strategy and structure which appear to make firms vulnerable to recessionary pressures.

Feedback to the labour market

Textbook stories of competition typically focus on the effects that competition has in the particular market where it occurs. However, most professional economists are familiar with the proposition that the effects of competition in one particular market can often be felt up and down the value chain.[12] Many of the most obvious costs of recessions are observed in the labour market, as unemployment rises and wage growth slows (although some believe that these costs are more apparent than real). One of our goals in what follows is to examine how firms adjust their headcount, looking at whether they do so gradually in a way that smooths out their response to recessionary shocks (as is the supposition of many applied econometric models of employment dynamics), or by making a small number of very large, discrete changes. We will also examine the degree to which firms try to use changes in wage costs to ameliorate the effects of shocks and cushion the degree to which jobs are cut, and we will try to identify the major determinants of these choices.

More subtle changes in labour markets may also occur in recessions as shifts in the relative bargaining power of management and unions alter working practices and industrial relations structures.[13] Further, shifts in perceived bargaining power affect the willingness of individuals to join unions and of firms to recognise them. One of our goals in what follows is to chart in some detail the kinds of structural changes in labour market and industrial relations activity which occur in recessions. In particular, we intend to look at how recessionary pressures affect the degree of union membership, union recognition and the incidence of plant level wage bargaining in firms.

Innovation

One of the longest and least satisfactory debates in economics is that which surrounds the question of what the right climate for innovation is. Much of the discussion in the literature has been concentrated on the Schumpeterian hypothesis, which suggests that large firms with at least some monopoly power are likely to be more innovative than firms in very competitive industries.[14] Many of these arguments turn on the ability of monopolists to finance risky R&D from retained (supernormal) profits, or to appropriate the full benefits of their innovations by limiting spillovers. The case is not, however, clear cut, since firms who operate in protected markets often lack an incentive to act quickly and decisively, and large firms are often overcautious and bureaucratic. Clearly some competitive pressure is likely to stimulate innovative activity, but it is equally clear that extreme adversity (such as one might encounter in a very competitive market) may be inimical to innovation. Very hostile environments are often thought to make firms too short-sighted and to starve them of the resources they need to innovate successfully. Further, problems of appropriation may be aggravated in competitive markets to such a point that firms lack the incentive to innovate. One of our goals in what follows is to take a slightly oblique look at these issues by looking at the association between adversity and innovative activity, focusing in particular on the innovative performance of firms which are more or less severely affected by recessionary pressures.

A second debate that has long occupied the attention of those interested in the determinants of innovation is the extent to which innovative activity is sensitive to market forces. In part, the question turns on whether innovation is supply-pushed or demand-driven.[15] This debate often resonates with those Schumpeterians who believe that a 'gale of creative destruction' is unleashed during a recession. For many, this process is stimulated by waves of innovation created by adverse market conditions, while some believe that the linkage between innovation and demand gives rise to long waves in economic activity.[16] These are big issues which we will make little progress in resolving here, but we will at least try to explore how the timing of decisions about new product and process innovation is affected by recessionary pressures. Further, if innovations are, in fact, affected by cyclical pressures, then it is interesting to ask whether variations in innovative activity over time are initiated by certain types of firm. It is not hard to believe that innovative firms are different from other types of firms, and one of our goals here is to try to identify the kinds of firms (if any) which bring forward product and process innovations in recessions, and link these choices to the other kinds of strategy choices which they make.

The plan

The substantive results of this project are reported in Chapters 3–6, which focus on company performance in the recession, the responses made by firms to recessionary pressures, the effects of the recession on industrial relations structures and labour market activity and the effects of the recession on innovative activity. These chapters are preceded by a discussion of our data and some of its properties, and followed by a brief summary and some speculations on the effects of extreme adversity on company performance. The meat of our results is contained in Chapters 3 and 4, while Chapters 5 and 6 pursue narrower, more specialised issues.

The book is based on a survey which we carried out in Spring 1993 involving a sample of large UK firms. Although the recession was believed by some to have ended at least six months earlier (this view has become more persuasive with the benefit of hindsight), it was certainly fresh in people's minds when we sent out our questionnaire. Some of its effects were still being felt by our responding firms when they received our questionnaire, and many of them were still responding to recessionary pressures. Chapter 2 sets out how the survey data was collected and describes the questionnaire survey we used to generate the data. After discussing the nature of our sample and its possible biases, we digress to examine several features of the data which form a useful background for what follows (in the second and third sections of the chapter). This includes information on the organisational and ownership structures of the companies in our sample, and information on firms' perceptions of the recession.

Representative firm models typically used by macroeconomists create the impression that all firms suffer in downturns, an impression reinforced by the tendency of journalists to concentrate almost exclusively on major corporate collapses and associated counts of job losses in the depths of recessions. This view of the effects of recessions on companies is not consistent with the data and, in Chapter 3, we document what actually happens to companies in recessions. The most notable feature of this data is the widening of performance differences between firms which occurs as the economy turns down. We explore this in several ways, and over a longer time scale than the few years surrounding the Major-Lamont recession. We also examine subjective and objective measures of performance, and use them to identify firms which appear to be particularly vulnerable to recessionary pressures. Finally, we look at the characteristics of firms who went into receivership or liquidation in the recession, and show that they are very similar to those of severely affected survivors.

Chapter 4 concentrates on how firms respond to recessionary pressures.

We start by identifying a broad range of different responses which firms could make, and progressively narrow in on the specific actions which most of them actually took. As it turns out, most firms focused on cutting costs by shedding labour, closing establishments and freezing wages. We also examine investment decisions, looking at decisions to abandon, postpone or bring forward a range of investments in tangibles and intangibles, and decisions to change company organisational structures. The data suggest that most firms change the structure of their organisations fairly often, but recessionary pressures are not the most important driver of such changes. Notable differences in the incidence of organisational change between small and large firms exist, although some of these may reflect particularly fragile organisational structures or certain types of ownership structure. More surprisingly, most firms do not slash investments in intangibles, and a large number of them bring forward investments in new products or processes.

Chapter 5 traces the effects of the recession back into the labour market. We examine how firms cut jobs, and whether wage adjustment and employment shedding are substitutes. In fact, the first impression that one gets from the data is that the two responses are complements and not substitutes. Further, it turns out that the probability that a firm will do either (or both) is affected (amongst other things) by the degree of unionisation. Possibly more interesting are the changes in labour market practices and institutions induced by the recession. Thus, we will also explore whether union membership, union density and structures of pay determination changed in the recession, and how such changes affect long-term trends in the UK's industrial relations system. In most cases, the data suggest that the recession did little to (or little more than) hasten developments stretching back over a decade or more.

Chapter 6 begins by using the literature and other empirical work to identify the role that demand plays in decisions to do R&D and introduce new products and processes. Although it is hard to be absolutely sure, our reading of the data is that innovative activity is driven by changes in demand, not the other way round. This said, the relationship between demand and innovative activity is not strong, and predicting when new inventions will be implemented is not easy. We then return to our data on investment decisions, and concentrate on identifying innovating firms; that is, those who brought forward product and process innovations in the recession. We examine the complementary investments which they made and try to identify the characteristics which distinguish them from other firms. This turns out to be a difficult task, and our work yields only the modest conclusion that innovators are firms which were not extremely badly affected by the recession. Indeed, many of them thought that the recession was over.

Finally, the themes of the book are tied together in the conclusion in Chapter 7. After summarising our results, we close with some speculations on recent popular versions of the pit-stop theory of recessions, asking the question: *Do firms emerge from recessions leaner and fitter?* Although this question is almost impossible to answer (many firms certainly emerge leaner from recessions), the overall impression we have from examining the data is that the kinds of changes which recessions induce often appear to be more destructive than constructive (closing establishments, shedding jobs). Further, the kinds of changes which almost certainly contribute to sustained long-term growth (changing organisational structures, upgrading plant and equipment, introducing new innovations) are not, on the whole, driven in a major way by recessionary pressures. The analogy between diets and vigorous exercise on the one hand, and recessions on the other is, it seems, a poor one.

2 The recession survey

The questionnaire and sample

The work reported in this book is based on a questionnaire survey conducted in the Spring of 1993. The object of the exercise was to examine how firms were coping with the recession. We attempted to explore a range of issues which are usually addressed only in case studies, but to do so by collecting data on enough firms to support generalisations about the effects of the recession on the population of large UK firms. The strategy behind the data collection exercise was to construct a sampling frame which provided quantitative (that is, balance sheet) data for all responding firms, and use the questionnaire to generate further qualitative information on the firms in the sample. This resulted in a database containing qualitative and quantitative data (stretching back up to fifteen years in many cases) on each member of a fairly large sample of firms, together with quantitative data on the population from which they were drawn.

The questionnaire itself was fifteen pages long. It contained 32 detailed questions and provided space for respondents to elaborate on their answers (this rarely generated useful information). The package that we sent to the firms is reproduced in full in the Appendix at the end of this book. The questions were divided into three broad sections: **The Effects of the Recession, Human Resource Management** and **Company Organisation.** The first section asked firms how severely they were affected by the recession, what their major problems had been and how they responded to the recession. The second section asked a number of detailed questions about the composition of their workforce, the methods they used to shed jobs, trade union recognition, bargaining level and their usage of wage freezes. Finally, the third section asked questions about the structure of ownership, the longevity

19

Table 2.1 Company survival and survey response: all firms live and trading independently in 1990

| | Responded to survey | | |
	No	Yes	Total
Live and Independent in 1993	1488	578	2066
Live but Taken Over	132	20	152
In Receivership or Liquidated	104	7	111
Untraced	27	0	27
All	1751	605	2356

Note: An additional 13 companies responded to the survey but destroyed the company identification code. 605 + 13 = 618, the total number of responses we received. Of the 605, 12 had poor financial accounts data, and also excluding the 7 failed firms yields a sample of 586.

of the CEO, company structure, changes in structure and the methods used to implement these changes.

The survey was carried out in the Spring of 1993, following a pilot on a sample of 70 unquoted firms undertaken in October 1992. The first set of questionnaires was mailed out in December 1992, and two follow-up mailings (to non-respondents) were undertaken in early February and in late March. The sampling frame was the EXSTAT database of large UK companies, which contained 2,356 contactable companies identified as trading independently in 1990. The three mailings generated 293, 170 and 155 usable replies respectively, adding up to a total of 618 replies.

Table 2.1 summarises how our sample of 611 constructed itself from the 2,356 firm sampling frame. It also shows the incidence of failed firms in the frame, and among respondents and non-respondents. Seven replies were received from companies who were in receivership or became so shortly after replying (111 firms from the sampling frame as a whole ceased trading, and a further 27 companies could not be traced). This yields a sample of 611 surviving companies out of 2,215 (a response rate of 28 per cent). Of these surviving firms, 152 were taken over during the period, including twenty which responded to the survey. Of the population of 2,215 surviving firms, 2,110 had company accounts data of reasonable quality for 1989, and 586 of them were among our respondents (also 28 per cent, as it happens). The difference between the 611 and the 586 samples is composed of thirteen responding companies which destroyed the identification code used to match the survey responses to the EXSTAT data, and a further twelve respondents with poor financial accounts data. We also received 43

Table 2.2 The size distribution of respondent and non-respondent firms, by 1989 sales

Sales (thousands)	% of responding firms	% of non responding firms
1–4,999	5.0	4.6
5,000–9,999	6.5	5.7
10,000–49,999	29.4	25.9
50,000–99,999	20.0	20.1
100,000–499,999	25.9	30.0
500,000+	13.3	13.7

Note: In the main, sales are dated 1989; 1990 is used when 1989 information is missing.

polite refusals to participate and one rude one. A further 47 partially answered questionnaires were also received but were not utilised in this book.

The most obvious feature of the EXSTAT database which might give rise to an unrepresentative sample of UK firms is that it is dominated by relatively large firms. EXSTAT does include some small firms, but they are under-represented: 45 per cent of EXSTAT firms employed 1,000 or more workers and only 6 per cent employed less than 50 (in 1989). However, only 13 per cent of all UK firms employed 1,000 or more workers, while 40 per cent employed less than 50. Our respondents employed 3.19 million people in 1989 (or about 5,200 employees on average), equivalent to 14 per cent of UK employment (18 per cent if public sector employment is excluded). Table 2.2 shows the size distribution (in terms of sales) of responding and non-responding firms. Nearly 60 per cent of our sample had sales in excess of £50m in 1989, and most of them generated turnover in the region £10m–500m: 13 per cent had sales in excess of £500m, and only 5 per cent had sales below £5m. That is, they were neither small firms, nor overwhelmingly large. The average turnover of respondents was £384m (for non-respondents, it was £399m). The size distribution of non-responding firms was almost identical to that of respondents, and both distributions were also very similar when size was measured by employment. Judged by size alone, the sample seems to be a reasonably random draw from the EXSTAT sampling frame.

In fact, it is hard to detect any important source of non-representativeness of our respondents relative to non-responding firms. Table 2.3 shows the industry breakdown of responding firms. This was broadly representative of that of the economy as a whole, although our sample appears to

Table 2.3 The breakdown of responding and non-responding firms by industry

Industry	Responding		Non-responding	
	No of firms	Per cent	No of firms	Per cent
Agriculture etc.	2	0.3	7	0.5
Energy	19	3.2	71	4.8
Chemicals	57	9.7	125	8.2
Engineering	111	18.9	272	17.9
Other Manufacturing	102	17.4	281	18.5
Construction	34	5.8	77	5.1
Retail etc	133	22.7	376	24.8
Transport	20	3.4	42	2.8
Business Services	80	13.7	195	12.8
Other Services	26	4.4	60	4.0
Unidentified	2	0.3	11	0.7
Total	586	100.0	1519	100.0

have a slight over-representation of engineering firms and a slight under representation of firms engaged in retailing. Again, the distribution across sectors of respondents and non-respondents seemed to be very similar. In much the same vein, Table 2.4 shows that responding and non-responding firms had similar pre-recession growth rates, profits to sales ratios, change in profits to sales ratios, debt assets ratios and cash liabilities ratios. If anything, responding firms were just a little more profitable, and they entered the recession in slightly better financial shape than non-responders.

Needless to say, the EXSTAT database has a number of limitations in addition to its restricted coverage of small firms, and these need to be borne in mind in what follows. First, our version of EXSTAT ended in 1990. We updated our data for all matching companies using on-line computerised databases of company accounts, such as Datastream. This was done on company name, sales and employment for an overlapping period to guarantee the match. However, this updating restricts the available information available to key variables such as sales, employment, profits and debt related measures. Second, EXSTAT has its own industry coding which can not be easily or reliably matched with the Standard Industrial Classification. This was again taken from other on-line databases, but is available only for firms trading in 1993. Hence, we cannot match industry data to firms who disappeared prior to 1990. These two problems mean that some of our analysis of the determinants of vulnerability and responses to the

The recession survey

23

Table 2.4 The financial characteristics of responding and non-responding companies

Variable	Responding		Non-responding	
	Mean %	Cases	Mean %	Cases
Growth rate of real sales, 1986 to 1989	54.16	516	53.92	1349
Operating profits/sales, 1986	12.63	524	12.28	1384
Operating profits/sales, 1989	14.37	583	14.01	1505
Change in operating profits/ sales, 1986–9	01.19	522	01.27	1384
Total debt/total assets, 1986	15.79	533	16.67	1409
Total debt/total assets, 1989	18.09	585	19.46	1517
Cash/current liabilities 1986	19.25	532	19.88	1409
Cash Current Liabilities, 1989	19.69	583	17.46	1518

Note: Years containing missing information for 1986 are replaced by 1985 or 1987. Missing information in 1989 is replaced by 1988 where available. T-tests of differences in means reject the hypothesis that the means are different across respondents and non-respondents except for Cash/Current Liabilities 1989, where the difference is just significantly different from zero at the 10 per cent level (t=1.67).

recession will necessarily be somewhat more limited than we would have liked.

The major problem with virtually all panels of data on firms is survivor bias. The rate of attrition over time even of quoted firms in the UK is rather high, and this means that samples of survivors are often rather small subsets of the population of firms of interest. What is worse, they are usually not randomly selected subsets. This creates a problem whenever important determinants of performance are also important determinants of the probability of survival, since their effects on performance may be confounded with their effects on survival. For example, if large firms are both more profitable than small firms and less likely to be taken over, then samples of surviving firms will contain a disproportionate amount of large firms and the correlation between size and profitability computed using them will understate the true effect of size on profitability.

To get a handle on the issue of survivor bias, it is useful to look at differences in characteristics between survivors and non-survivors (we will analyse the determinants of failure in more detail in Chapter 3). Table 2.5 displays the financial characteristics of firms between 1986 and 1989 according to their survival status in 1993.[2] Two points on the table are worth

Table 2.5 The financial characteristics of companies by survival status

Variable	Live	Taken over	Failed	Untraced
Growth rate of sales, 1986–9, %	52.45	73.73*	77.09*	42.51
Sales 1989 (millions)	£417	£202*	£107*	£162
Operating profits/sales, 1986, %	12.50	12.87	10.34	9.08
Operating profits/sales, 1989, %	14.12	14.65	9.03*	9.10
Change in operating profits/sales, 1986–9, %	1.17	1.98	0.60	0.11
Total debt/total assets, 1986, %	16.55	16.19	18.53	15.14
Total debt/total assets, 1989, %	19.12	22.53**	27.48*	20.21
Cash/Current Liabilities, 1986, %	19.92	19.39	20.95	21.76
Cash/Current Liabilities, 1989, %	18.87	17.49	15.28	12.39

Notes: Mean values are shown. Years containing missing information for 1986 are replaced by 1985 or 1987. Missing information in 1989 is replaced by 1988 where available. * indicates significant differences with base live group at a 5 per cent level, while ** indicates significant differences at a 10 per cent level only.

noting. First, companies that were taken over or went into receivership were substantially smaller and faster growing in terms of sales between 1986 and 1989 than other firms. In particular, takeover victims were half the size of survivors but grew 40 per cent faster between 1986 and 1989; failed firms grew nearly 5 per cent faster still, but were just over half as small again. They also held more debt and were less cash rich in 1989 (but not in 1986). It is clear that the financial position of failed firms weakened considerably (relative to both survivors and takeover victims) between 1986 and 1989. The second observation of interest is that survivors had profit margins which were slightly lower than takeover victims, but 21 per cent larger than the margins of failed firms. Further, performance differences between firms were much larger in 1989 than 1986: the margins of survivors were 13 per cent higher in 1989 than 1986 on average, while those of failed firms were just under 15 per cent lower in 1989. As we shall see shortly, these differences deepened as the recession took hold.

Although it is rather rough and ready, these observations suggest that analyses of the determinants of firm performance using data only on surviving firms may have two sources of potential bias. First, profit margins, firm size and firm growth are all likely to be potentially important determinants of survival, given both the size and significance of the differences between survivors and failed firms in these respects. As a consequence, it is important to keep in mind that effects on survivors associated with these characteristics (for example, on their vulnerability to recessions) may not accurately reflect their effects on all firms, survivors and non-survivors alike. Second, there are interesting differences between failed firms and those who were taken over. The latter look much more like survivors (at least when judged by financial performance), except with respect to their size and pre-recession growth rates. It is, therefore, hard to believe that they were, in general, failing prior to being taken over. This suggests that there may be two rather different forms of selection evident in the data, failure and take-over, which claim rather different types of victims. Further, since mergers and acquisitions are typically procyclical, while liquidation rates tend to vary countercyclically, it seems likely that selection criteria may vary somewhat over the trade cycle.

Organisation and ownership structures

The questionnaire was designed to generate information which would help us to understand why some firms were more vulnerable to recessionary pressures than others, and to help explain why they responded as they did to these pressures. Many of the most interesting features of firms do not make it on to financial balance sheets (and, therefore, into the EXSTAT database). To make any real progress, it is necessary to generate as much of this data as possible. We, therefore, tried to generate data on several determinants of firm performance that are not usually available from traditional data sources. Two of the most important of these are company organisational structure and ownership structure. Since the information we uncovered on these exogenous variables is interesting in its own right, it is worth a digression to report what we found.

The simplest distinction that one can draw between different types of company structures is between functionally organised companies who structure themselves around specific activities (sales, finance, marketing, production and so on), and more decentralised structures built up from more or less independent operating divisions. Among firms with decentralised structures, a further distinction is often made between holding companies and divisionalised firms. The former are often loosely coordinated collections of disparate groups of companies held together by finan-cial control mechanisms under the supervision of a weak central headquarters which does not try to act as an internal capital market. Divisionalised firms often contain more industrial logic, their constituent companies act as profit centres and their central headquarters often play a more active role in strategy formulation and act as an internal capital mar-ket, reallocating cash between divisions.[3] Functionally organised firms are often specialised, with narrow product ranges, while holding companies are often diversified conglomerates.

We asked firms to indicate which *basic organisational structure most closely resembled that of your company*, using the stylised diagram repro-duced as Figure 2.1. We focus on the sample of surviving firms with reasonable accounts data for consistency of presentation. 188 firms (32 per cent of the sample) identified themselves as functionally organised, 202 (35 per cent) were holding companies and 150 (28 per cent) were divisionalised in one form or another (16 per cent and 12 per cent respectively). In addi-tion, 28 (5 per cent) could not fit their firm into the diagrammatic structures given. Firms organised as holding companies controlled about 9.3 operat-ing companies on average, and 36 of them (20 per cent) controlled more than ten operating companies. Divisionalised firms controlled 9.9 operat-ing companies on average, but only 22 of them (15 per cent) controlled more than ten.

These numbers are something of a surprise. Previous work on the organi-sational structure of UK firms suggests that the representation of functionally organised firms in the top 250 dropped from 11.7 per cent in 1964–6 to 7.5 per cent in 1970–72.[4] Projecting forward leads one to ex-pect only a very small number of functionally organised firms in 1990 (say, less than 5 per cent of the sample), and certainly far fewer than we have observed. There are two differences between our survey and previous work which may account for at least some of this discrepancy. First, our sample is much broader than most of those used in the past, and includes many more (relatively) small firms. Since the incidence of divisionalisation in-creases with firm size, this almost certainly means that our survey will show a lower overall percentage of divisionalised firms than one focused only on the top 250 firms in the UK.[5] Second, our sample includes non-manu-facturing firms, and functional structures are relatively more common in retailing and services, while divisionalised structures are relatively uncom-mon in these sectors.[6] As a consequence, our sample is more likely to produce a low estimate of the extent of divisionalisation than samples drawn exclusively from manufacturing. Despite this, it is hard to believe that the creation of large divisionalised organisational structures which

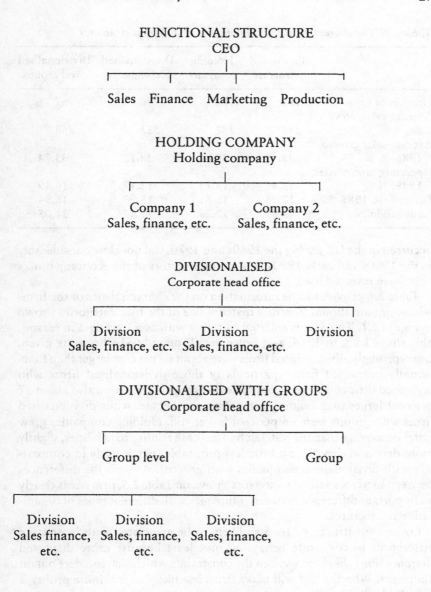

FUNCTIONAL STRUCTURE
CEO

Sales   Finance   Marketing   Production

HOLDING COMPANY
Holding company

Company 1   Company 2
Sales, finance, etc.   Sales, finance, etc.

DIVISIONALISED
Corporate head office

Division   Division   Division
Sales, finance, etc.   Sales, finance, etc.

DIVISIONALISED WITH GROUPS
Corporate head office

Group level   Group

Division   Division   Division
Sales finance,   Sales, finance,   Sales, finance,
etc.   etc.   etc.

Figure 2.1 *Stylised company structures*

Table 2.6 *The characteristics of companies with different structures*

	Functional structure	Holding company	Divisionalised company	Divisionalised and groups
Number of firms	162	182	86	67
Average sales, 1989, £m	312	332	522	868
Average sales growth, 1986–9, %	35.32	44.86	38.12	35.74
Operating profits/sales, 1989, %	13.85	13.13	13.17	16.49
Debt/assets, 1989, %	17.75	18.51	18.93	16.94
Cash/liabilities, 1989, %	18.85	17.26	19.37	21.05

occurred in the UK during the 1960s and 1970s did not slow considerably in the 1980s and early 1990s, and in some sectors of the economy it may even have reversed itself.

Table 2.6 provides some information on the characteristics of the firms whose organisational structure matches one of the four categories shown in Figure 2.1. The data is collated for firms with accounts data in reasonable shape back to 1986, and hence details on only 514 firms are given. Unsurprisingly, divisionalised firms were about 67 per cent larger than functionally organised firms (particularly those divisionalised firms who organised their constituent companies in groups). They were also about 57 per cent larger than holding companies on average, while divisionalised firms with groups were 66 per cent larger still. Holding companies grew faster on average than the rest, but had less cash relative to liabilities, slightly more debt and they were a little less profitable (particularly in comparison with divisionalised companies with groups). As with the differences between survivors and non-survivors shown on Table 2.5, firm size is clearly an important difference between companies with different types of organisational structures.

Ownership structures are also likely to be associated with interesting differences in corporate behaviour, not least because more dispersed shareholding is likely to weaken the constraints which shareholders put on managers. Whether this will make firms less likely to maximise profits is disputable, but it will certainly increase the independence which managers enjoy. We requested firms in our sample to describe their ownership structure, asking them to put themselves into one of five categories shown on Table 2.7. Although it is difficult to be absolutely sure, we are inclined to rank these structures from left (*UK Subsidiary*) to right (*Highly Dis-*

Table 2.7 *The characteristics of companies with different ownership structures*

	UK subsidiary	Majority stake by directors	Significant minority by directors	Other significant minority	Highly dispersed
Number	96	116	74	36	195
Average sales, 1989, £m	353	94	165	334	757
Average sales growth, 1986–9, %	21.48	35.46	55.68	46.67	42.44
Operating profits/ sales, 1989, %	10.89	12.22	14.57	15.94	15.45
Debt/assets, 1989, %	15.91	16.29	17.11	17.53	20.30
Cash/liabilities, 1989, %	12.68	19.44	21.27	26.22	19.17

persed) in terms of increasing dispersion of ownership and, therefore, as increasingly likely to identify firms where managers have considerable discretion.

The data suggest that nearly two thirds of the firms in a sample are likely to have shareholders powerful enough to affect manager's decisions: 18 per cent of the sample were subsidiaries of foreign firms, 35 per cent were controlled by directors who had a majority or a *'significant'* minority stake (21 per cent and 14 per cent respectively), 7 per cent were controlled by a non-board member who held a *'significant'* minority stake, and about 37 per cent had a *'highly dispersed'* share ownership. Three per cent reported another ownership pattern or were unable to place themselves in one of the categories given. These figures are also a little surprising, since most other work has suggested a higher degree of ownership dispersion among leading UK firms than is apparent in our sample.[7] Again, part of this difference is almost certainly due to the higher proportion of small, non-manufacturing firms in our sample, but it is not at all clear just how important these differences are.[8] Given the rather imprecise ownership dispersion categories which we have used, it would be imprudent to infer from our data that shareholding has actually become more dispersed in the UK over the last decade (although this may actually have been the case).

Table 2.7 provides some information on the characteristics of firms in our sample with different ownership structures. Three observations are worth making on the data displayed on the table. First, firm size is apparently the simplest and most important discriminator between firms with different ownership structures. Firms where the directors own a majority or a substantial minority holding were substantially smaller than other firms (on average, they were one-eighth the size of firms whose shareholdings were 'highly dispersed'), and firms with a significant minority stake held by directors were 50 per cent (or less) the size of other firms. Needless to say, firms with 'highly dispersed' ownership structures were, on average, much larger than the rest. Second, UK subsidiaries stand out from the rest. They grew much more slowly than all other types of firm and they reported much lower profit–sales, debt–assets and cash–liabilities ratios. Some of these differences are appreciable: compared to (say) firms with 'highly dispersed' ownership structures, their growth rates were 50 per cent lower, profit margins were 40 per cent lower, debt was 28 per cent lower and cash 50 per cent lower. Third, firms whose ownership is highly dispersed are often thought likely to be managerially controlled and, therefore, more willing to sacrifice profits for growth. This, of course, should make them vulnerable to takeover, and may increase their susceptibility to recessionary pressures. Plausible as these arguments seem to be on a priori grounds, they appear to be inconsistent with the data shown on Table 2.7: 'highly dispersed' firms were, on the whole, more profitable than the rest, and they were amongst the fastest growing firms in the sample. Nevertheless, their size and rapid rate of growth prior to the recession may have created management problems which are likely to have been exacerbated by the loose control that highly dispersed shareholders have over managers. The contrast with foreign owned subsidiaries is particularly marked in this respect, and it will be interesting to observe whether either type of firm turns out to be particularly vulnerable to recessionary pressures.

Finally, it is interesting to cross-classify organisation and ownership structures, and the basic data to do this are shown on Table 2.8. The most prominent feature of the data is that functionally organised firms and holding companies had more tightly held ownership patterns than divisionalised firms. Only 19 per cent of the firms with a 'highly dispersed' ownership structure had a functional structure, much lower than the 40 per cent for divisionalised firms; 54 per cent of the subsidiaries of foreign firms were functionally organised, much higher than the 20 per cent of all firms. Holding companies were common among all ownership types except foreign subsidiaries. These observations are much as one might expect, and are almost certainly driven by firm size: large, diversified firms tend to have dispersed ownership structures and, to be controllable, they are often divisionalised. Smaller firms are frequently specialised and, as a consequence, they are often functionally organised and controlled by a small group of (occasionally family related) shareholders. The most important

Table 2.8 Organisation and ownership structures

per cent

	Functional structure	Holding CO	Divisionalised CO	Divisions and groups
UK subsidiary of foreign CO	54.4	14.6	9.7	11.7
Majority stake held by current directors	40.3	41.9	7.3	8.9
'Significant' minority stake held by current directors	32.5	42.2	19.3	3.6
'Significant' minority stake held by one individual or institution	28.6	23.8	31.0	9.5
Ownership 'highly dispersed'	19.2	38.8	21.9	18.3

variation is, therefore, between a holding company structure and a divisionalised one for dispersed ownership, and between functional and holding company for the less dispersed ownership types. Foreign firms are heavily reliant on the functional structures.

Perceptions of the recession

Our main interest in this project is to understand how companies cope with recessionary pressures. Needless to say, the first step in this process is to ascertain how severely they have been affected by the recession, and why. As a by-product of collecting this information, we discovered a number of things about firms' perceptions of the Major-Lamont recession of the early 1990s, and it is worth a (second but final) digression to set this information out.

The feature which stands out most in the data recording firms' perceptions of the recession is how selective the effects of the recession are. Table 2.9 displays answers to the survey question: *How severely has your company's operations been affected by the recession?* As it happens, only 18 per cent of responding firms felt that they had been 'extremely severely' affected, and another 39 per cent felt that they had been 'severely' affected. At the other extreme, 21 firms (3 per cent) felt that they had 'not (been af-

Table 2.9 The impact of the recession on individual firms and expected duration of these effects

per cent

	All	Over already	Over in <6 months	Over in 6–12 months	Over in 12+ months
All	100	8	8	35	49
Extremely severely	18	2	5	30	63
Severely	39	2	6	36	56
Moderately	41	10	11	39	41
Not at all	3	94	6	0	0

fected) at all'. That is, less than one in five firms were very badly affected by the recession, while only just over 50 per cent of the responding firms in our sample felt themselves to be seriously affected by the recession one way or the other. This, of course, means that one of every two firms responding to our survey did not report major, or even serious, disruptions to their operations. Some firms suffer acutely during a cyclical downturn, but others continue to prosper.[9] We will return to this observation in Chapter 3 below.

Our survey was conducted in the Spring of 1993 at a time when many people (and particularly the members of John Major's government) were beginning to feel that the effects of the recession were proving to be frustratingly persistent. We asked our sample of firms the question: *When do your expect the recession to be over for your company?*. The data discussed in Chapter 1 suggested that the recession had already ended by the Spring of 1993. However, nearly half of the responding firms believed that the recession would continue for longer than a year (that is, persist beyond the Spring of 1994), while 35 per cent felt that it would persist for another 6 to 12 months. Unsurprisingly, those firms who were '*extremely severely*' affected by the recession were much more likely to believe that it would last longer than a year (63 per cent) than those who were only '*moderately*' affected (41 per cent). Most of those who were '*not at all*' affected thought that the recession was over (93 per cent). Finally, as noted above, we collected our data over three waves of mailings, and the percentage of respondents who thought that the recession would last more than a year was 51 per cent, 52 per cent and 42 per cent respectively, with 85 per cent, 86 per cent and 74 per cent respectively stating that they believed that the recession would last longer than 6 months. This is consistent with a slight lifting of the recessionary gloom during the Spring of 1993, but it does not reflect a revolutionary change in perceptions.

Table 2.10 The effect of the recession on company operations

per cent

'How has the recession affected the following aspects of your company's trading position in the years 1990–1992?'

	Seriously	Somewhat	Not at all
Decline in UK sales	47	39	10
Decline in o/seas sales	10	30	35
Excess capacity	24	42	20
Excess inventories	8	37	38
Excess indebtedness	16	36	37
Cashflow constraints	23	42	30

Note: The residual is 'no answer'; that is, 4 per cent of the respondents failed to answer the first question.

Table 2.10 tries to pinpoint the source of recessionary pressures by identifying the effects of the recession on each company's trading position. Even a cursory glance at the table suggests that the problems created by the recession were perceived to be demand led, but it is a failure in domestic and not world demand which caused most problems for respondents.[10] Although the recession caused some problems associated with excess capacity, excess inventories and cashflow constraints, it seems clear that the main perceived source and driving force of the problem is lack of domestic sales. More than a third of the respondents were not affected at all by a decline in overseas sales, excess inventory or excess indebtedness, while 30 per cent were not affected by cashflow constraints and 20 per cent were not affected by excess capacity. Virtually all of the firms who felt that they had been 'extremely severely' affected by the recession experienced a 'serious' decline in UK sales, but 43 per cent of them also cited excess indebtedness, 50 per cent cited excess capacity and 62 per cent cited cashflow constraints as serious problems as well.

Another way of assessing the importance of factors other than the decline in UK sales is to look how many firms reported serious effects without citing UK sales: of the firms not facing a 'serious' decline in UK sales, 19 firms stated 'declines in overseas sales' were a serious problem, 23 firms cited 'excess capacity', 10 cited 'inventories', 29 cited 'excess indebtedness' and 33 cited 'cashflow constraints'. Although the number of firms stating these as problems was not high, they are the most important independent sources of serious problems apart from the collapse in domestic demand (and, of course, any other factors omitted from the questionnaire).

It is possible to be more specific about firm's perceptions of why the de-

Table 2.11 The sources of the recessionary pressures

per cent

'More specifically, which of the following factors have been a source of your company's current problems (tick as many options as is appropriate)?'

	Very important	Some importance	Not important
(a) Macroeconomic conditions			
High interest rates	43	37	15
High exchange rate	22	41	29
Low consumer confidence	50	32	13
Worldwide recession	29	45	21
International competition	17	32	43
Falling land/building prices	23	22	48
(b) Decisions within the firm			
Expansion of company through merger or acquisitions before 1990	16	16	59
Over expansion of range of products or services provided before 1990	6	19	65
Over investments in plant/buildings before 1990	9	21	57
Insufficient product or process innovation	6	25	57
Poor control of costs	11	37	44
(c) Actions of other firms			
Increased competition in your product market	38	43	14
Innovations introduced by rivals	6	35	48
Non or late payment by customers (ie bad debts)	16	48	29
Credit limits by banks etc.	15	25	51

Note: The residual is 'no answer'; that is 5 per cent of respondents did not check any of the three boxes associated with 'high interest rates'.

cline took place and whether firms can identify the transmission mechanisms which affected their firm in particular. Table 2.11 displays the answers which we received to the question: *which of the following factors have been a source of your company's current problems?* 82 per cent of the respondents cited at least one of the six *'macroeconomic conditions'* listed on the table, while 50 per cent cited one of the four *'actions of other firms'* and only 29 per cent cited at least one of the five *'decisions within the firm'* factors. Unsurprisingly, nearly all of the *'severely'* and *'extremely severely'* affected firms cited macroeconomic conditions as being *'very important'*. Again, unsurprisingly, the two macroeconomic conditions which seem to have caused most concern were *'low consumer confidence'* (50 per cent of the respondents thought that this was *'very important'*) and *'high interest rates'* (43 per cent). Only 15 per cent of the respondents thought that either of these was *'not important'*. High exchange rates did not appear to be a major source of concern and, indeed, only 29 per cent of those firms who exported at least 5 per cent of their output cited high exchange rates as a problem. Similarly, the effects of the *'world wide recession'*, *'falling land/building prices'*, and *'international competition'* were not generally perceived to be *'very important'* by more than a third of our respondents, and as many as 43 per cent thought that *'international competition'* was *'not important'*.

The sense in which firms feel responsible for what happened to them in the recession is, it seems, surprisingly limited. Only 170 firms cited one or more of the *'decisions within the firm'* factors and only 6 of the 586 respondents cited only *'decisions within the firms'* factors. Nearly half our sample (and frequently more) thought that the five *'decisions within the firm'* factors were *'not important'*. Of those who did perceive internal problems, *'overexpansion through merger'* was the main response: 41 firms cited only *'expansion of the company through merger'*, while another 54 cited this factor among others. By contrast, 37 firms cited *'over expansion of product range'* amongst other things, 54 cited *'over investment in plant'* among other things, 34 cited *'insufficient product or process innovation'* among other things, and 62 cited *'poor control of costs'* among other things (20 firms cited only *'poor cost control'*). A significant minority of firms, therefore, thought that at least some of the seeds of the problems experienced in the early 1990s had been sown in the mid to late 1980s merger boom.

Firms seem to be somewhat more likely to blame others for the problems which they encountered during the recession than themselves: 303 firms cited at least one of the four *'actions of other firms'* listed on Table 2.11 as being *'very important'*. Given that the recession was perceived by the responding firms as being due to a failure in demand and not a financial crisis, it is not too surprising to discover that only 87 of them cited *'credit limits by banks'* as being *'very important'* (32 cited it as the only source of their problems), only 94 cited *'non or late payment by customers'* (32 cited only this factor) but that as many as 221 cited *'increased competition in (their) product market'*. *'Innovations introduced by rivals'* do not seem to have caused important problems for many firms, and more firms thought that payment problems by customers or credit limits by banks were *'not important'* than thought that they were *'very important'*. Since a decline in the level of domestic sales is likely to induce a closer interdependence between rival firms scrambling for a slice of the shrinking pie, it is very difficult to distinguish between *'increased competition in ... product market(s)'* caused by new entry or an increase in imports and that caused by a large decline in the demand for the products of a static or declining number of supplying firms. Our informal sense of these replies is that most of the firms in our sample who felt the pressure of increased competition did so because demand had shifted in, and not because supply had shifted out.

In summary, only just one in five firms said that they were *'extremely severely'* affected by the recession, while just under one in two were unaffected or only *'moderately'* affected. Managers' perceptions of the origins of the recession as it affected their firm were clearly driven by what happened in UK markets rather than any worldwide phenomena. The prime source of difficulty arose from a collapse in UK sales which was widely believed to have been caused by low consumer confidence, and may also have been exacerbated by intense competition from rivals in shrinking markets. Exchange rates were not generally perceived to be a problem, and few firms felt the impact of the world wide recessionary pressures which some politicians saw as the source of problems in the UK. Interest rates were thought to be one of the more important factors helping to create the recession, but their impact on most firms appears to be of second order of importance. Some badly hit firms, however, suffered from high debt, excess capacity and cashflow problems, and high interest rates mattered more for them. Only a small minority of firms felt that a financial squeeze was the only major source of their problems, although nearly two thirds of those firms who indicated that expansion through merger or acquisition before 1990 caused them problems also cited debt or cashflow as serious problems (this was despite record levels of company debt prior to the onset of the recession). It follows that most of the data generated by our survey records the response of firms to a fall in demand rather than an inflation in costs or a financial squeeze. Thought of as a natural experiment, the data describes events surrounding a sharp, sudden and sustained inward shift in the demand faced by leading UK firms.

3   Company performance over the business cycle

Introduction

Some economists (and not a few lay commentators) think that recessions are periods of cleansing in which the supply side of the economy is restructured and, as a consequence, rejuvenated. Sometimes described in grand Schumpeterian terms as a process of 'creative destruction', this view depicts economic growth as unfolding over time in a series of disorganised spurts (possibly associated with waves of product or process innovation), each of which is followed sooner or later by a period of retrenchment and rationalisation. Implicit in this view is the supposition that economies become overstretched and resources are progressively misallocated in cyclic upswings, a state of affairs which may limit both their duration and amplitude. Excessive queues or order backlogs, labour mismatching or hoarding, an enhanced tolerance of slack and, perhaps, an excessive lengthening of the life of capital equipment are all observable manifestations of this resource misallocation and they are, therefore, also likely to be the kinds of phenomena which disappear in recessions as the economy cools.

At the most casual level, this view is roughly consistent with the fact that growth is not a smooth process when viewed either at the macro or the micro level: GDP has a large random walk component in its evolution, and much the same applies to the growth of sales turnover or the assets of individual firms. Further, variations in the level of aggregate output or GDP cannot be easily or unambiguously decomposed into secular and cyclical variations over time: that is, the data are hard to reconcile with the view that the long-run secular expansion of an economy (or a firm for that matter) is independent of cyclical fluctuations in economic activity.[1]

If it occurs at all, the process of recession-induced structural change operates through one of two mechanisms: first, failing firms exit and make

37

room for the entry or expansion of more dynamic and efficient firms and, second, continuing firms increase their dynamism and efficiency by restructuring and refocusing their activities.[2] That is, the process of cleansing is essentially a selection process in which stagnant and relatively inefficient firms are selected against, and dynamic and relatively efficient firms are favoured. There are several ways in which selection might occur. A collapse in demand may trigger a price war which reallocates market share in favour of firms who are in control of their costs, and may even lead to the exit of those firms who are unable to operate economically. Alternatively, relatively inefficient firms who fail to generate adequate cash flow or persuade their bankers to provide risk capital may be starved of finance capital. This reduces their ability to compete through product and process innovation, and it may make it difficult for them to maintain a steady stream of positive net investment in plant and equipment (much less in human or technological knowledge capital). Needless to say, restructuring not only depends on the push to exit which some firms receive, but also on the pull of entry offered to others. That is, the pressures which induce less efficient firms to exit will be considerably strengthened if entry and the desire of managers of more efficient plants to expand their operations does not fall during recessions.[3]

In studying how well selection processes restructure firms and the markets that they operate in, two interesting issues arise: first, *does sufficient diversity in performance between firms exist to enable selection to occur?* and, second, *what are the criteria which underlie selection decisions?* Our goal in this chapter is examine these issues. The next section focuses on the differences in company performance which arise during recessions, examining the variability of company performance over the cycle, the persistence of performance within companies over time and the skewness in the effects of the recession on firms. We then examine the selection mechanism itself, looking at what makes particular (surviving) firms more or less vulnerable to recessionary pressures. Finally, we try to identify the factors which seem to determine which firms are forced into receivership. We also consider whether these criteria differ from those associated with failure in more prosperous times.

Performance differences between companies

The view that economies undergo an unusually high degree of restructuring during recessions rests on the premise that selection pressures are stronger during recessions than in booms. This will be true only if the diversity in corporate performance which selection feeds on widens countercyclically, meaning that differences in performance between firms diverge in recessions but converge in booms. For this to happen, at least some firms must be much more severely affected by recessionary pressures than others.

Measuring corporate performance

To make any sense of these hypotheses, it is necessary to start by choosing an appropriate measure of company performance. For most economists, the natural first choice is some index of productive efficiency and, in a perfectly competitive (or contestable) market in which firms have no control over price and relatively little latitude to differentiate their products, this is probably the only interesting measure of performance that one would want to consider. However, when firms have some degree of market power and are protected by barriers to entry, excess profits generated by super-competitive prices can compensate for an inability to control costs. Indeed, it is not always clear that a profit maximising firm with market power will choose to operate at the bottom of its average cost curve, and managers who face loose governance structures may tolerate high levels of slack in their firm's operations. Further, efficiency in raising revenue from the sale of a particular good or service can (but does not always) reflect a superior service provided to consumers and, in this sense, it may be no less welfare increasing than cost savings (particularly if these are not passed on to consumers in lower prices). All of this suggests that the right kind of measure of performance might be value added or profitability.[4]

There are, of course, a number of well known problems with measuring profitability.[5] One which causes concern in the current context is the question of whether measures of current (accounting) profits accurately reflect the underlying, long-term competitive ability of a company. The problem is that while low levels of current period profitability can be caused by the inability of a firm to cope with adverse cost or demand shocks, they can also be caused by the actions which firms take to deal with these adverse shocks. This is a subject which has generally been discussed under the heading of adjustment costs; that is, transitory costs associated with changes in firm size, strategy or structure. One particularly important source of adjustment costs is that associated with managerial constraints.[6] To operate effectively, managers must work as an integrated team: goals must be widely agreed, routines established and tacit knowledge shared. As even the best managed firms expand in scale and scope, this team becomes more and more stretched and must expand. However, introducing new members can be disruptive: new managers must be socialised, routines must be adapted to new people and new circumstances and, possibly most important, new managers must absorb much of the tacit knowledge base on which the firm's current operations continue to rely. Since tacit knowledge transmission is at the centre of this problem, the only way for new managers to learn is from old managers, and this means that the latter must take time off from their operational duties to train new managers. This, of course, increases the stretch on the existing, incumbent management team, lowering managerial effectiveness in the short run.

The bottom line is that the use of profit margins as a measure of corporate performance is a natural choice, not least because it is reasonable to believe that profitability (and not cost efficiency or productivity) will be the most important criteria which markets use to select between firms. However, profitable firms are not always efficient, and current levels of reported profits may not always reflect underlying long-run levels of profitability. This means that a strong correlation between profits and selection does not imply that only efficient firms are rewarded by the market, while a weak correlation does not necessarily mean that selection is random or does not follow 'the fundamentals'. As a consequence, although it is interesting to ask whether profits are linked to selection pressures, it would be imprudent to read into such correlations any inferences about the efficiency of market selection.

The variability of corporate profitability over the economic cycle

Probably the clearest and most commonly observed feature of company profitability over the cycle is that, on average, most companies perform less well in recessions than in booms. More interesting and much less well documented is a second observation, namely that the dispersion in company profit margins rises markedly in recessions. The top panel in Figure 3.1 shows the distribution of profit margins for about 2,300 large UK firms over the period 1971–93.[7] Average profit margins varied procyclically (with highs of 12.8 per cent and 13.2 per cent in the boom years of 1973 and 1988, and lows of 9.3 per cent and 11.4 per cent in the trough years of 1981 and 1991), but showed no clear trend: margins in 1988 and 1989 were roughly in line with those in 1972 and 1973. More interesting is the middle panel, which reveals that there was a trend rise in the standard deviation of profits across firms, with peaks in the two recession years of 1981 and 1991. Indeed, dispersion seems to have risen in these two recessions, and never returned to pre-recession levels (not withstanding the long boom in the 1980s). The bottom panel of the figure brings the top two panels

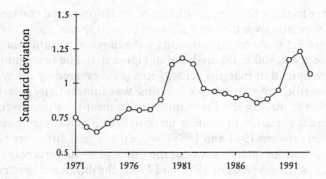

Figure 3.1 *Distribution of operating profit margins 1971–93: mean, standard deviation, and coefficient of variation*

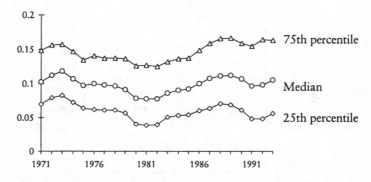

Figure 3.2 *Quartile distribution of operating profit margins 1971–93*

together to show that the coefficient of variation varied countercyclically, rising secularly over time in a series of uneven spurts.

Figure 3.2 provides information on the range of variation in profit margins for the 2,300 firms analysed in Figure 3.1. The first point to note is that the spread of margins across firms (as measured by the width of the interquartile range) at any point in time was substantially greater than the variation in median (or, for that matter, in mean) margins over time. The maximum variation in median margins was 5 percentage points (which occurred between 1981 and 1989), while the typical difference between the top and bottom quartiles was of the order of 8–10 percentage points. In the two recession years of 1981 and 1991, the difference between top and bottom quartiles was 8.8 and 10.4 percentage points, while in the boom years of 1973 and 1989 it was only 7.5 and 8.5 (about 20 per cent lower). Further, the interquartile range was strongly countercyclical, with firms at the bottom of the distribution falling further in percentage terms in recessionary periods. The 25th percentile margin fell from 5.7 per cent to 3.9 per cent between 1979 and 1981, and from 6.9 per cent to 4.8 per cent between 1989 and 1991. At the upper 75th percentile, margins only fell from 13.6 to 12.6 per cent and 16.7 to 15.4 per cent in the same periods. Thus, between 1989 and 1991 operating profit margins declined by 2.1 percentage points at the 25th percentile, by 1.5 points at the median and by 1.3 points at the 75th percentile. All of this is summed up in Figure 3.3, which shows that the log of the 75/25 percentile differential displayed a cyclical pattern overlaid on a strong upward trend, confirming once again that profits grew more dispersed over the period.

Average profitability falls in recessions at the same time as the variance of profitability rises mainly because recessionary pressures are concentrated

Figure 3.3 *Log of the interquartile range of operating profit margins 1971–93*

on a relatively small number of firms whose profits (sales, employment, and so on) fall very steeply. In fact, it is firms in the bottom quartile of performance (measured by profit margins, changes in sales or changes in employment) who bore the brunt of the recession, as Table 3.1 shows. This worst performing 400 or so firms lost nearly £3bn in profits, £8bn in sales and shed (net) 800,000 jobs between 1989 and 1991.[8] Total profits declined from £117bn to £96bn (a drop of £21.3bn) for these firms as a group, but the 10 per cent of firms who experienced the biggest fall in operating profits saw their profits collectively decline by £27bn. The 10 per cent best performing firms actually increased profits by £10bn. In fact, the total decline in profits among those firms whose profits actually fell was £32.3bn, and 84 per cent (92 per cent) of this fall was accounted for by the worst performing 10 per cent (20 per cent) of firms.

Much the same skewness is evident in the data on sales and employment, even when one focuses only on survivors. Although the 1,764 firms reporting accounts in 1989 and 1992 cut employment by 473,000 (from roughly 8.5 million to about 8.0 million) or by about 5.5 per cent, only 55 per cent of these survivors shed labour. The total number of jobs shed by all job losers was 1.05 million, of which 886,000 (84 per cent) were shed by the 175 firms who suffered the biggest net decline in employment. The quintile shedding most jobs accounted for 94 per cent of all job losses, while the 86 firms who went into receivership before reporting 1992 accounts only added 135,000 lost jobs to the total loss. That a small number of severely affected (surviving) firms bear a disproportionate share of recessionary pressures is a very robust result.[9]

It is important to note that the fact that poorly performing firms perform

Table 3.1 Profits, sales and employment declines across 2,100 UK firms 1989–91

	Change in operating profits (£000)	Change in sales (£000)	Change in employment (000)
Bottom decile	−27000	−71800	−725
2nd decile	−2864	−10200	−77
3rd decile	−1280	−4398	−31
4th decile	−1650	−2084	−12
5th decile	−319	−896	−3
6th decile	−113	−190	1
7th decile	16	440	7
8th decile	222	1774	20
9th decile	806	5109	60
Top decile	9899	40100	400
Total net change	−21300	−42100	−361
Total change of those with declines	−32300	−89600	−849

Note: The employment changes are for 1989–92 wherever possible, which is for about 1,700 of the cases.

Table 3.2 Correlations in profit margins over time[*]

Year	5 Years	10 Years	15 years	20 Years
1971	0.76	0.60	0.53	0.40
1976	0.65	0.52	0.38	-
1981	0.60	0.42	-	-
1986	0.54	-	-	-

Note: For a balanced panel of 480 firms continuously observed over the period 1971–1991.

extremely poorly in recessions does not mean that the profitability of firms who were weak performers prior to the recession plummeted in the recession. The data we have just examined says only that some firms were badly affected by the recession. The next question to ask is whether there is any link between pre-recession profitability and profitability in the recession.

The persistence of corporate profitability

Most theories about the dynamics of profitability turn on the hypothesis that entry, exit and other forms of competitive feedback induce an autoregression in profits: high profits today attract entry, which leads to profits being bid away tomorrow. The evidence, however, is that fluctuations in profitability over time are rather modest and are driven by random or idiosyncratic factors. Most firms report persistently high or low levels of profitability over relatively long periods of time, and the variation in profits between firms at any point in time is typically much larger than that within firms over time.[10] Unless the dynamics of movements in profitability change over the cycle, one's expectation is, therefore, that firms who perform poorly in recessions are likely to have been performing poorly just prior to the recession and, similarly, firms who perform well just prior to a recession ought to be relatively unaffected by recessionary pressures (*ceteris paribus*).

To explore this hypothesis, we put together a balanced panel of 480 firms who operated continuously over the period 1971–91. Table 3.2 shows the correlations in profit margins between cross sections of this panel over successive 5 year periods. Typically, the correlation between profits in t and profits in $t+5$ was about 0.6 (although it was higher in earlier years, and declines in size by about a third over the sample period). This initial five year correlation gradually declines as the period over which the correlation is computed widens. For example, profits in 1971 were correlated to profits in 1976 with a coefficient of 0.76, to profits in 1981 with a coefficient of 0.60, to profits in 1986 with a coefficient of 0.53 and to profits twenty years later with a coefficient of 0.40. Figure 3.4 plots the annual correlations between profits in 1971 and subsequent years. The sharpest decline in the correlation was in the first few years, after which the correlation declined mainly in the recession periods 1979–82 and 1989–92. That is, although profits show a tendency to converge to a norm, the correlation with lagged profits is weakest in recessionary periods.[11] Note that even after twenty years, profits are still highly autocorrelated, meaning that high/low levels of accounting profitability tend to persist for long periods of time.

Another way to describe the persistence of profitability which we have just observed is to look at transition matrices which describe movements within the ranking of firms over time. Table 3.3 shows the quartile distribution of the panel of 480 survivors over the period 1971–89. Just over half of the survivors from the top quartile in 1971 were still in the top quartile of firms ranked by profitability in 1989 and, similarly, just under half of the firms in the lowest quartile of performers in 1971 were in the

Figure 3.4 *Correlations of operating profit margins between 1971 and subsequent years for a balanced panel of 480 firms*

Table 3.3 *Quartile distributions of profit margins 1976–89*

per cent

1976	1989			
	Q1	Q2	Q3	Q4
Q1	53.4	19.9	17.6	9.2
Q2	22.3	39.2	25.4	13.1
Q3	8.7	35.0	32.8	23.5
Q4	6.8	8.7	35.9	48.5

lowest quartile in 1989 and, of course, some of them failed (mobility amongst the middle two quartiles was rather higher than at these two tails). Only 9 per cent of top quartile performers ended up in the bottom quartile in 1989, while only 7 per cent of the bottom performers in 1971 rose to the top quartile in 1989. However you look at it, rankings of firms by profitability are fairly stable over time.

The two observations that: (i) differences in profits between firms tend to persist over time and (ii) that the dispersion of profits differences between firms widens in recessions, are, on the face of it, a little difficult to reconcile with each other. It seems clear that the post-recession profit margins of some firms are much less closely related to their pre-recession profitability than are the profit margins of other firms, but the question is whether this is true only for poorly performing firms. One way to explore this question is to use profit rankings in a non-recession year (like 1976) to identify the

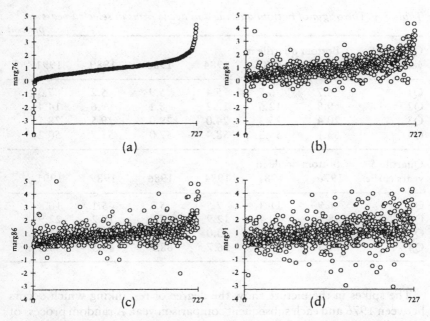

Figure 3.5 *Plot of operating profit margins in selected years against the rank of a firm's margin in 1976*

movements of firms within the distribution of profits in recessionary periods.[12] Figure 3.5 plots the profitability of firms in two non-recession years, 1976 and 1986 (panels (a) and (b)), and in two recession years, 1981 and 1991 (panels (c) and (d)), against each firm ranked by profitability in 1976. In 1976, margins and rank form a smooth, upward sloping profile with two tails of much steeper slopes reflecting the existence of a few outlying firms at either end of the distribution. The steepness of the slope reflects the difference in margins between the best and worst performing firms in the sample. Observing this plot over time yields some clues about which firms (identified by their position in the distribution of 1976 rankings) experienced major changes in performance over time. For all but the outliers, the slope of the plot remains a fairly shallow upward sloping line in 1981, 1986 and 1991. Declining persistence is represented by the upward sloping line converging to the line on the vertical axis at average profits. This occurs quickly for the outliers, but is generally true over time for the whole distribution.

Table 3.4 *The origin of bottom quartile and decile firms in selected years*

per cent

Quartile 5 years earlier	Bottom quartile in					
	1976	1981	1984	1986	1989	1991
Q1	6.7	6.7	5.4	5.9	5.2	7.3
Q2	9.8	12.6	12.2	8.1	9.6	14.4
Q3	20.4	25.3	24.0	29.0	29.5	28.1
Q4	63.1	55.3	58.4	57.0	55.7	50.2
Quartile 5 years earlier	Bottom decile in					
	1976	1981	1984	1986	1989	1991
Q1	6.9	11.3	7.5	5.3	5.1	10.8
Q2	8.1	10.4	12.9	7.9	10.2	22.9
Q3	13.8	31.1	23.0	18.1	19.3	31.1
Q4	71.3	47.2	56.7	68.9	65.5	35.2

The spikes in the picture show the degree of re-ranking which occurs between 1976 and each subsequent comparison year. A random process of re-ranking would lead to progressive increases in the degree of spikiness over time. What we actually observe is that there are particularly noticeable increases in spikiness in 1981 and 1991 relative to 1986 (in which the observations are relatively tightly packed along the average profit level). The prominent downward spikes in the distribution identify firms which were particularly severely affected by the recession (relative to the 1976 performance), while the upward spikes identify firms whose performance improved substantially. What is particularly interesting about Figure 3.5 is that the observations with profits below zero (that is, firms making losses) occur throughout the entire distribution, meaning that both high and low ranked performers in 1976 were severely affected by the recessions in 1981 and 1991. What is more, at least some firms from both ends of the distribution seemed to prosper (relatively) even as others suffered. Clearly, then, recessions increase the dispersion of performance partly by inducing an apparently unsystematic re-ranking of firms according to past performance which considerably weakens the correlation between pre-recession and within-recession profitability.

Much the same story emerges from an inspection of Table 3.4, which shows the performance quartile which a firm was situated in five years earlier for the worst performing firms in selected years. Unlike Figure 3.4, Table 3.4 uses all firms available in the year pairings and, hence, does not ignore firms which subsequently die. Interestingly enough, in the recession years of 1981 and 1991, the proportion of bottom quartile firms that were also in the bottom quartile five years earlier was much lower than in other years.[13] Similarly, a slightly higher proportion of firms transited from the top quartile into the bottom quartile in 1981 and 1991, reflecting the scrambling phenomena discussed earlier.[14] The lower panel repeats this exercise for the more acutely distressed firms in the bottom decile. The points made above apply far more strongly to these firms. The most extremely distressed firms in the recession years are drawn from across the previous distribution. More than twice as many firms moved from the top quartile to the bottom decile between 1986 and 1991 than was the case between 1984 and 1989.

In a sense, Table 3.4 summarises much of what we have discussed in the last few paragraphs: while there is a tendency for firms who were performing badly just prior to the recession to perform very poorly during the recession, it is also the case that an unusually large number of firms who performed well before the recession saw their performance deteriorate suddenly and very substantially when recessionary pressures began to build up.

Finally, it is worth asking whether recessions create scars in the sense that firms which suffer particularly badly in one recession also suffer badly in subsequent recessions. Given how long profit differences between firms persist, it is natural to think that poor performers in 1981 would also be poor performers in 1991 (if, that is, they survived until 1991). Set against this, however, is the possibility that firms which survive severe recessionary pressures only do so because they transform their operations and upgrade their capabilities. In this case, those firms which were badly affected by the recession in 1981 are likely to find themselves amongst the top performers in 1991. In fact, the data seem to be inconsistent with both of these views.

Figures 3.6 and 3.7 show that it is not the case that some firms are inherently vulnerable to recessions, and have repeatedly bad experiences in successive recessions (given that they survive both). Figure 3.6 plots profits margins in 1991 against profitability rankings in 1981. The degree of scrambling (as reflected in the spikiness of the distribution) is large compared to that shown on Figure 3.5, and it is obvious that substantial re-rankings occurred up and down the distribution. Figure 3.7 plots the change in the performance of firms between 1979–81 against that experienced by the same firms between 1989–91. Clearly there is no relationship between profit changes in the two recession periods.[15] Only 15 per cent of the bottom decile of the distributions in the two distributions were common to both years. This is greater than would occur in a random ten-year overlap (but not by much), and is less than the similar ten-year overlap

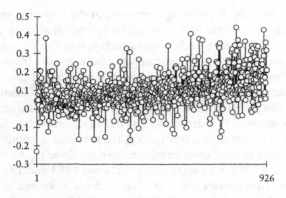

Figure 3.6 *Changing pattern of profit margins between 1981 and 1991*

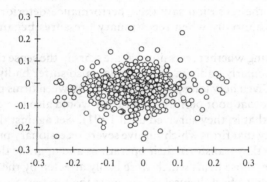

Figure 3.7 *Changes in profit margins 1979–81 and 1989–91*
Note: For a panel of 926 firms

which we observe in non-recession years (the overlap between the two boom periods centred on 1976 and 1986 is just over 40 per cent). All of this said, it is important to recall that attrition bias would produce very similar effects (badly affected firms in 1981 would have had either to improve or fail), so these conclusions should not be pushed too hard.

In summary

All of this seems to point to two stylised facts about company performance over the trade cycle. First, average profitability varies procyclically while the variance of profitability varies countercyclically (and has also been increasing fairly steadily over the past 20–25 years). These obviously interrelated movements in the first two moments of the distribution of company profitability are caused by the very large but very selective concentration of recessionary pressures on a relatively small number of firms. Second, while differences in profitability between companies typically persist for long periods of time, recessions do seem to induce apparently random (that is, unrelated to previous profitability) reorderings in the ranking of firms by profitability. These re-rankings are not extensive enough to make the statement that 'profits persist' a seriously inaccurate description of the data, but they are noticeable in a diminution in the size of parameters describing the degree of persistence and in an increase in apparent statistical noise which occurs during recessions. This scrambling phenomena is, however, sufficiently strong to obliterate any correlation between poor performance in successive recessions, and to noticeably weaken that between pre- and within-recession profitability.

The fact that the dispersion in company performance increases in recessions provides grist for the selection mill to grind on. However, the scrambling phenomena we have observed raises some questions about what exactly drives selection pressures. Whatever it is, it is not strongly related to pre-recession profit margins, and this means that accounting profitability is unlikely to be a useful summary statistic describing the strength of selection pressures facing firms as they enter a recession. This raises the interesting question of whether any pre-recession characteristics of firms are closely correlated with selection, or whether market selection operates apparently at random.

What makes firms vulnerable to recessionary pressures?

If recessions really are part of a cleansing process in which some firms expand and prosper while others decline or exit, then it is important to examine the selection criteria which markets apparently use to discriminate between firms. That is, it is important to understand what makes some firms suffer unduly in a recession while other firms prosper. To make progress on these issues, it is necessary to identify likely discriminating variables, explain why they seem to matter, and then develop measures of vulnerability.

The natural first step in examining selection criteria is to focus on current levels of profitability, and ascertain the degree to which it is poor profit performers who contract or exit and high profit firms who expand.

Although it is clear from our earlier discussion that poor pre-recession performers sometimes perform poorly during recessions, it is also evident that recessionary pressures can severely affect firms whose profits were high prior to the recession. All of this suggests that, in practice, selection criteria may well involve more than just relative profitability, or, to put the matter another way, current levels of (accounting) profitability are unlikely to be a sufficient statistic of performance for the selection process. This is something of a puzzle and it creates some problems of interpretation. Profits are a residual which emerges from the balance sheet when all the relevant cost and demand side pressures have recorded their influences on a firm's operations. Why many of them should have any independent influence on selection is not clear, unless, of course, the construction of measures of accounting profits somehow distorts the effects of these independent factors. For example, if Penrose effects mean that firms who grow rapidly face substantial adjustment costs, one expects this to be recorded in their current profits, and one would not expect to observe measures of corporate growth exerting an independent effect on a firm's vulnerability to recessionary pressures.

The difficulty is that while measurement error might explain why factors other than profits appear to affect selection, it is also possible that other factors affect selection because profits are not the prime determinant of selection pressures; that is, because the selection process is not, in some sense, efficient. This means that it is very hard to mount a deeply persuasive test of the proposition that market selection pressures are efficient in the sense of being driven mainly by profit criteria. The natural way forward is to focus on the more modest question of the sufficiency of profits as a measure of selection criteria, and ask which additional observable characteristics of firms play a discernible role in discriminating between firms which are badly affected by recessionary pressures and those which are not. Thinking in terms of a standard regression model, this suggests comparing a null hypothesis that only profits matter against an alternative which suggests that certain features of a firm's operations affect selection above and beyond the effect which they have via profitability.

There are, perhaps, four additional sets of factors which might affect selection above and beyond current profitability. The first is that firms may encounter transitory adjustment costs as they respond to current and recent past cost and demand shocks. These costs will lower current levels of profitability, but do not necessarily indicate that the firm suffers from a fundamental competitive weakness. As we noted above, such costs of adjustment may be associated with very rapid growth and diversification. Given the relatively unimpressive success rate of most mergers, one also expects that acquisition oriented firms may suffer unusually high costs of growth, and this may also be associated with relatively high levels of debt. Thus, we expect variables such as pre-recession growth rates, acquisition activity and debts relative to assets or cash all to be positively associated with the probability that a firm will suffer during recessions.

The second set of factors which might affect the vulnerability of firms to recessionary pressures is the diversity of their operations and, in particular, the degree to which their operations are diversified internationally. Although there appears to be some degree of synchronicity in business cycles between countries, it is nevertheless the case that firms who produce or export abroad may find that declines in demand in one market are somewhat offset by events in other markets (this will also be true for domestically diversified firms facing sector specific shocks). Further, multi-market firms often have access to information in one market which can be usefully applied in other markets, giving them a competitive advantage relative to specialised firms. Finally, multi-market firms may find it easier to collude or otherwise maintain pricing discipline in the face of a contraction in demand, and this may enable them to avoid some of the effects of recessions which firms in more competitive, less disciplined markets face.

The third set of factors which might affect how firms perform during recessions is firm size. For those who believe that economies of scale are an important source of competitive advantage, firm size is often the most important determinant of a firm's competitive ability. Large firms are also likely to have better access to short-term crisis finance than small firms, and this is reflected in the very much higher failure rates of small firms. However, size cannot be the whole story, since it also matters how well an enterprise is managed. It is not difficult to think of many large firms which failed (meaning, in most cases, that they were taken over and broken up) because they were poorly managed. At least two factors are of importance in this context: governance structure and organisation structure. Firms in which ownership is separated from control often have difficulty in monitoring the activities of managers who, as a consequence, may sacrifice the firm's long- run future for their own shorter-term gains. Similarly, some types of organisational structure make it easier for top managers to keep in touch with the markets which they serve than others.

Fourth and finally, recessions do not have the same effects on all firms because the nature of their operations differ. Export intensive firms will be more vulnerable to recessionary shocks transmitted via exchange rates than to declines in domestic demand, while heavily capital intensive firms or those selling consumer durables will be more susceptible to recessionary shocks transmitted through high interest rates than others. Finally, some sectors are more inherently cyclical than others and may, in addition, experience seasonal cycles which exacerbate or ameliorate cyclical shocks.

In order to examines how selection works, it is necessary to identify the effects of selection. At first sight, the solution to this problem seems to be pretty straightforward. Natural selection operates by rewarding those individuals or species who are favoured by selection with a more rapid rate of population expansion than individuals or species who have been selected against. This suggests that one might identify the effects of selection by looking at how it affects the investment decisions of firms: those firms favoured by selection will invest and grow, while those which have been selected against will be unable to carry out their investment plans. Indeed, they may be forced to scrap plant and equipment instead of expanding, or they may be forced to run down their stocks of consumer goodwill, human capital or technological knowledge capital. Either way, their long-run growth will be less than it might otherwise have been and, indeed, they may even end up ceding market share in the short run. However, the problem with this approach is that to assess just how important selection pressures are, one needs to be able to establish a clear counterfactual describing how much investment might have occurred in the absence of selection pressures, something which is not always easy to do. Some firms will invest less than others in any given period regardless of selection pressures simply because their investment opportunities are less rich, and this might easily be confused with adverse selection pressures.

Two alternative procedures might be used to alleviate this problem and enable us to say something about selection criteria. The first involves examining the subjective impressions of managers about how badly their firms have been affected by recessionary pressures and using these as measures of the strength of selection pressures. Since these subjective perceptions can often play a large role in investment decision making, they may prove to be an accurate index of the effects of recessions on investment behaviour and, therefore, on future growth.[16] This is the route we will take in the next section. The second way forward is crude but reasonably powerful, and that is to associate selection pressures with survival or failure. Firms that are selected against fail, while the rest survive. The problem with this is that it is probably too simple. There is no doubt that at least some surviving firms are very severely affected by recessionary pressures, and are forced to make numerous changes to their current and planned future operations because of the competitive environment which they find themselves in. Using survival ability as a criteria will, therefore, lead one to understate the effects that selection has on firms. It does, however, provide a useful consistency check on results obtained using subjective performance measures. One way or the other, we will explore this route later.

Table 3.5 *Subjective measures of vulnerability to the recession and accounting profitability*

Severity of recession on firm	Median profits, 1991	Median change in profit, 1989–91	Median percentage change in employment, 1989–92
'Extremely severe'	0.033	−0.044	−0.219
'Severe'	0.090	−0.024	−0.073
'Moderately severe'	0.134	−0.006	0.032
'None at all'0.131	0.010	0.044	
All respondents	0.099	-0.018	-0.047

Note: Profit margins are defined as profits before tax plus depreciation and interest payments divided by sales.

The vulnerability of continuing firms

To construct subjective measures of well-being, we asked the companies which responded to our survey: '*How severely have your company's operations been affected by the recession?*', offering them a choice of ticking boxes labelled: '*extremely severely*', '*severely*', '*moderately*' and '*not at all*' (see Chapter 2 above). 18.3 per cent of respondents felt that they were '*extremely severely*' affected by the recession, 38.5 per cent were '*severely*' affected, 39.9 per cent were '*moderately*' affected and 3.4 per cent felt '*not at all*' affected. Our view is that the measures of well-being are likely to conflate the current and expected future states of the firms' operations. Managers whose firms are performing poorly and who do not see a solution will proclaim themselves to be much more severely affected than those managers whose firms are currently performing as poorly, but who do see a way forward. Similarly, managers of profitable firms who foresee major problems facing them in the near future will proclaim themselves to be less well off than managers of equally profitable firms facing blue skies.[17]

Using the subjective evaluation of recessionary pressures provided by the 614 respondents to our survey, Table 3.5 provides *within recession* information on median profitability, median changes in profits and median employment change for responding firms affected in different ways by the recession. It is clear from the table that the ranking of firms by subjective assessment is very similar to the three apparently 'objective' rankings. Firms that were '*extremely severely*' affected by the recession were noticeably less profitable than all others, and suffered much larger losses in profits and

Table 3.6 Characteristics of firms by severity of impact of the recession

	Extremely severely			Severely			Moderately		
	Median	Mean	Variance	Median	Mean	Variance	Median	Mean	Variance
Profit margin 1989	0.097	0.125	0.016	0.103	0.130	0.016	0.140	0.164	0.018
Average profit margin 1985–9	0.093	0.120	0.012	0.098	0.127	0.015	0.138	0.158	0.017
Debt/assets 1989	0.210	0.205	0.021	0.149	0.183	0.015	0.122	0.172	0.040
Cash/liabilities 1989	0.056	0.148	0.042	0.079	0.188	0.080	0.103	0.225	0.100
Sales 1989	56.3	160.3		79.5	398.8		64.9	500.6	
Growth in log real sales 1986–9	0.335	0.454	0.345	0.343	0.437	0.317	0.252	0.309	0.279
Prop. holding company	–	0.462	0.251	–	0.354	0.230	–	0.290	0.207
Prop. sales exported	0.0	0.09	0.027	0.10	0.18	0.046	0.10	0.22	0.067
Prop. foreign owned	–	0.125	0.110	–	0.175	0.145	–	0.187	0.152
Prop. 2+ acquisitions	–	0.269	0.198	–	0.327	0.221	–	0.190	0.155

Note: Based on a sample of 576 firms, of whom 18 per cent reported being 'extremely severely' affected by the recession, 38 per cent 'severely' affected, 40 per cent 'moderately' affected and 3 per cent 'not at all' affected. Those stating 'not at all' affected have been merged with the moderately affected for the purposes of this table.

employment at the beginning of the recession than other firms. Indeed, *'extremely severely'* affected stand out from all other firms in this respect: the difference between their performance and that of *'severely'* affected firms was larger than that between the latter and all other firms.[18] It is hard to resist the conclusion that these subjective perceptions do correspond to meaningful differences in performance between firms.

Table 3.6 displays some of the *pre-recession* characteristics of firms who were *'extremely severely'*, *'severely'* and only *'moderately'* affected by the recession. *'Extremely severely'* affected firms were less profitable, more indebted and less cash rich than other firms. They also grew more rapidly just prior to the recession and were more acquisition oriented than *'moderately'* affected firms (the differences between *'extremely severely'* and *'severely'* affected firms in these respects were very small). Finally, *'extremely severely'* affected firms were more likely to be holding companies, less likely to be foreign owned and were less export oriented than others.

Table 3.7 Ordered probit estimates of the severity in impact of the recession

	(i)	(ii)
Profit margin, 1989	0.7102 (0.4538)	0.6642 (0.4622)
Change in margin, 1986–9	0.3309 (0.6256)	0.1792 (0.6391)
Log(sales), 1989	0.0580 (0.0304)	0.0532 (0.0318)
Growth of sales, 1986–9	−0.2249 (0.0860)	−0.1323 (0.0902)
Cash/liabilities, 1989	0.4468 (0.1848)	0.3512 (0.1873)
Debt/assets, 1989	−0.1420 (0.2775)	−0.2671 (0.2833)
Exports as % of sales	–	0.0080 (0.0022)
Non-UK production as % of sales	–	0.0042 (0.0020)
Foreign owned	–	−0.0628 (0.1379)
Holding company	–	−0.1893 (0.1055)
Product range 2+ 2 digit SIC ind.	–	−0.0088 (0.1002)
Acquired 2+ companies, 1986–90	–	−0.1858 (0.1176)
Log Likelihood	−588.1	−573.2
Pseudo R2	0.0194	0.0443
Number of observations	521	521

Note: 'Extremely severely' affected = 0, 'severely' affected = 1, 'moderately' affected = 2, 'not at all' affected = 3. Standard errors are given in t-statistics in brackets after the estimated coefficient. This table is similar to that reported in Geroski and Gregg, 1986, but was drawn from regressions on a slightly different sample.

They were also just a little smaller than other companies. As we saw in Chapter 2 (and will see again shortly in the next section), these differences between extremely badly affected firms and others are similar to those between survivors and failed firms.

Needless to say, the amount which can be learned from Table 3.6 is a little limited, since it is not clear that all of the variation observed on the table is independent. Our null hypothesis is that pre-recession profitability will be a sufficient statistic of distress, and that most of the rest of the association between the other independent variables and vulnerability is caused by their association with profitability and does not reflect additional independent causal influences. To pursue this, one needs to examine multiple correlations, and Table 3.7 shows two regressions which explore the relation between the vulnerability of firms to a recession and their *pre-recession* characteristics. Regression (i) shows ordered probit estimates of a simple model which includes profit margins, changes in margins, firm size, firm growth, the ratio of cash to liabilities, the ratio of debt to assets as determinants of which of the four classes of well-being a firm's managers thought best described the current state of their operations. High pre-recession growth was positively and significantly associated with the severity of the impact of the recession on corporate performance, at least as perceived by managers, while size and the ratio of cash to liabilities were negatively associated with vulnerability (note that the ordered probit runs from 0 for *extremely severely* affected to 3 for firms *not at all affected* by the recession). Pre-recession margins, the change in margins and the debt asset ratio had the expected signs, but were not statistically significant. Regression (ii) adds six further potential explanatory variables, including export intensity, the intensity of foreign production, whether the firm is a holding company or foreign owned, how broad the firm's product range is and how acquisition active it was prior to the recession.[19] Of the original six independent variables, only firm size and the ratio of cash to liabilities remained significant; export intensity was negative and significantly related to vulnerability.

There are (at least) four interesting features of Tables 3.6 and 3.7 which are worth further comment. First, distress in the recession is not well correlated with pre-recession profitability or with changes in pre-recession profitability. As we noted earlier, the firms that find themselves in acute distress seem to be drawn from all over the pre-recession distribution of profitability and, while there is a clear tendency in the data for more profitable firms to be less severely affected by recessionary pressures, it is rather imprecise. Far from being a sufficient statistic, pre-recession profitability seems to be a rather weak predictor of distress. In no case is it possible to accept the null that only pre-recession profitability matters and, indeed, in many of the regressions which we ran, profitability was insignificant (even when many of the other exogenous variables were omitted). We did, however, detect a rather imprecise positive association between the historical variability of a firm's profits and its vulnerability to recessionary pressures.

Second, and following from this, it is actually fairly difficult to predict the vulnerability of firms to recessionary pressures using the twelve independent variables shown on the table. The inclusion of further explanatory variables and industry dummies did not help much and, indeed, we found it very hard to make accurate predictions about which firms were most likely to feel themselves to be *extremely severely* affected by the recession. The scrambling of the distribution of firms ranked by pre-recession performance in recession does apparently contain a relatively large random component. There is certainly too much intra-industry variability in how firms cope with recessionary pressures to make predictions of the inter-industry incidence of recessionary pressures which might be used to identify potentially vulnerable firms.

Third, both firm size and export intensity seem to be clearly associated with distress and, at least in the recession of the late 1980s, large export oriented firms seem to have been less vulnerable to recessionary pressures than smaller, more domestically oriented firms (this may reflect the fact that the origin of the 1991 recession was a collapse in domestic demand). Since ours is a sample of large firms, the rather modest sized size effect shown on Table 3.7 is likely to understate its true effect of size on vulnerability.[20] As we noted earlier, both governance and organisational structure may be as important as size and Table 3.6 shows that holding companies were over represented in the set of *'extremely severely'* affected firms, while foreign owned firms were less severely affected by recessionary pressures than others. The picture is less clear on Table 3.6, but it seems plain that there was at least a weak tendency for holding companies to be *'extremely severely'* affected. Although introducing other categorical variables reflecting governance or organisational structure did not improve the fit in regressions (i) and (ii), our impression of the data is that firms with tighter organisational structures (like functionally organised firms) and tighter governance structures (like foreign owned firms or those whose shareholdings were not highly dispersed) fared somewhat better in the recession than others, all else the same.

The fourth interesting feature of the regressions shown on Table 3.7 is the association between growth, acquisition, debt and cash. While high pre-recession growth rates were clearly associated with an enhanced vulnerability to recessionary pressures in regression (i), much of this effect seems to be picked up in regression (ii) by the acquisition variable. The two variables were positively correlated and growth (and also acquisitions) was weakly correlated to both the debt/assets ratio and the cash/liabilities ratio. Needless to say the cash/liabilities and debt/assets ratios were negatively related to each other. All of this suggests that rapid pre-recession growth makes firms vulnerable to recessionary pressures, particularly when it is driven by acquisitions and fuelled by high levels of debt. What is more, these effects seem to be related to company structure. Holding companies were more acquisition oriented over the period 1986–90, and they maintained higher levels of growth and debt. Finally, it is also worth noting that analogues of (i) which used data on *within recession* growth (that is, over the period 1989–91) rather than *pre-recession* growth (that is, over the period 1989–91) generally found positive and significant coefficients on growth rates. That is, firms that grew fast during the early phases of the recession generally proved less vulnerable to the recession than others.

Finally, it is worth noting that these results appear to be robust to a number of alternative specifications of the models shown on Table 3.7. We ran probit regressions identifying firms who were *'extremely seriously'* affected by the recession, and distinguishing them from all other firms. Since many of the differences between *'extremely severely'* and *'severely'* affected firms shown on Table 3.6 were large relative to differences with *'moderately'* affected firms, it is not surprising that probits distinguishing these two categories were somewhat more informative. Either way, these exercises produced the same qualitative conclusions as were drawn from Table 3.7. We also ran probits modelling the probability that the firm was in the bottom decile of profits in 1991, and found a negative and significant correlation with 1991 size and a positive and significant correlation with growth over the period 1986–9. Cash and debt were negatively and positively associated with the probability of being ranked at the bottom, but neither coefficient was significant. The inclusion of industry dummies in all of these regressions marginally improved the fit, but had a less than marginal effect on the estimated coefficients. We also included a count variable indicating the number of two digit industries the firm operated in, but it had a weak and imprecisely negative effect on vulnerability.

Which firms failed?

There are two reasons why it is important to extend the analysis of the last section to look at failing firms. First, failure is natural reflection of selection forces: firms that fail must have been especially vulnerable to the effects of recessions. At the very least, looking at failure provides a robustness check on the results obtained by examining vulnerable survivors. Second, focusing attention on only surviving firms runs the risk of generating attrition bias: that is, of confounding the effects of some variable (like firm size) on company performance conditional on survival with its effect on survival probabilities.

Failing firms

The decision to force a firm into receivership is likely to be driven by short term financial difficulties coupled with a pessimistic assessment of the long term prospects of the firm. As with all selection decisions, it is never clear in principle or practice how much weight is (or should be) put on short term financial distress. In addition, the decision to put a firm into receivership depends on an assessment of whether receivership is better than allowing the firm to trade its way out of distress. This may be constrained by the firm's size and its financial reserves, and it may depend on the firm's reputation based on its past performance. These observations suggest that many of the factors which might be relevant to determining a firm's vulnerability to recessionary pressures will, therefore, also be relevant to determining how likely they are to be put into receivership.

To explore these issues, we were forced to extend our data somewhat. This turned out to be easier than it seemed at first sight, since firms which cease reporting company accounts are not deleted from the EXSTAT database and, from 1987 to 1990, the reason for the exit is recorded in the EXSTAT database. Three categories can be (roughly) distinguished: those firms who are taken over by another company, those who go into administrative receivership or liquidation and those who are deleted from the EXSTAT sample for other or for unknown reasons. The exact year of failure is unknown, but we could sometimes observe the last recorded accounts year for each failed firm. However, from 1990 on, this data is not available, and we had to piece company histories together from a number of other sources of company information available in business libraries.

Tracking exit from recession to recession reveals that a little under half of all of the firms with accounts for 1981 were no longer trading independently by 1993. Table 3.8 shows the survival rate and timing of the exit for firms ranked by profitability in 1981. It is clear that more profitable firms survived longer, and the survival rate fell over time for all firms regardless of their initial 1981 profitability level. Further, the main difference in survival rates occurred in the first five years after 1981: the worst performers in 1981 were 50 per cent more likely to fail between 1981 and 1986 than all others, but after 1986 survival rates were roughly independent of initial levels of profitability. A t-test for equality of means of the death rate between 1981–7 being the same for the bottom decile relative to the rest of the sample was rejected with a t-statistic of 3.69 (with 2210 degrees of freedom). As the reason for death is unobserved, it is quite probable that this understates differentials in failure rates (since the ending of reported accounts at the top end of the distribution is likely to include more takeovers and mergers). To identify the principal cause of death, we need to focus on recent failures. 111 of the 2,353 firms alive in the EXSTAT sample in 1990 were identified as going into receivership or liquidation by 1993 (a failure rate of 4.7 per cent), while 152 were taken over and 27 were untraced. Of these, only 1993 companies provided usable 1990 accounts data and traced status for 1993. 100 of these firms went into receivership or were liquidated (also a failure rate of 4.7 per cent over 3 years).[21]

Unsurprisingly, it was the poor performers in 1990 (that is, in the early phase of the recession) who were most likely to fail. Of firms in the bottom decile of 1990 profit margins, 71 per cent survived until 1993, 18 per

Table 3.8 Survival rates of firms by operating profit margins in 1981

| | Last accounts reported | | | | |
	Survivors	1981–6	1987–9	1990–93	Unknown
Profit margin in 1981					
Top 50 per cent	55.8	25.2	12.8	6.0	0.2
Next 25 per cent	49.9	28.6	14.1	6.9	0.5
Next 15 per cent	51.7	25.7	14.8	6.3	1.5
Bottom 10 per cent	41.0	37.8	13.5	6.8	0.9

Table 3.9 Probit estimates of firms going into receivership 1988–90 and 1991–3

Going into receivership	1988–90		1991–3	
Profit margin <0 (t)	0.8805	0.7838	1.058	0.8927
	(0.1863)	(0.2005)	(0.1192)	(0.1303)
Profit margin >=0	0.3124	0.2500	0.2399	0.1645
but <0.03 (t)	(0.1608)	(0.1697)	(0.1775)	(0.1854)
Profit margin >=.03	0.2111	0.1639	0.2305	0.2248
but <0.06 (t)	(0.1499)	(0.1571)	(0.1619)	(0.1678)
Debt/assets (t)	–	1.0613	–	1.102
		(0.2863)		(0.2241)
Cash/liabilities (t)	–	0.0008	–	–0.2807
		(0.1845)		(0.1912)
Ln employment (t)	–	–0.1036	–	–0.0744
		(0.0336)		(0.0290)
Ln sales(t)– Ln sales (t–2)	–	0.1779	–	–0.0510
		(0.0754)		(0.1077)
Constant	–1.928	–1.512	–1.998	–1.712
	(0.0696)	(0.2506)	(0.0761)	(0.2234)
Sample size	1963	1963	2026	2026
Pseudo R squared	0.0375	0.0853	0.1034	0.1505
Log likelihood	–304.1	–288.3	–338.6	–320.6

Note: Time t is 1987 for the 1988-90 period and 1991 for 1991-93. t-2 is lagged two years from these dates. If information was not available for 1991, 1990 was used instead.

cent went into receivership, 8 per cent taken over and 4 per cent were not traced. However, 91 per cent of firms in the top half of the distribution survived, only 6 per cent were taken over, 2 per cent went into receivership and 1 per cent were not traced. Just over 40 per cent of all companies going into receivership were in the bottom decile of performers in 1990, but only 14 per cent of these firms were in the bottom decile in 1988. That is, *pre-recession* performance was much more weakly correlated with failure than *within recession* performance. By contrast, 87 per cent of live firms in 1987 survived until 1990, 3.6 per cent went into receivership, 6.2 per cent were taken over and 2.7 per cent deleted from EXSTAT. Of the bottom decile in 1987, 83 per cent survived up to and including 1990, with just 9 per cent going into receivership and 5 per cent being taken over.[22] Thus, being among the worst 10 per cent of companies ranked according to profits in a recession seriously increased the risk of death relative to being more profitable or relative to being amongst the worst performers in non-recession years.

Failure rates at any time are driven both by the number of loss making firms and by the differential mortality rates of loss makers. In 1987, 98 firms (4.5 per cent) reported negative operating profits and, in 1990, 175 (7.6 per cent) firms made loses. The failure rate was 13 per cent amongst these loss makers in 1988–90, but was a much higher 22.3 per cent in 1990–93 (similar failure rates exist at all other levels of profitability). The split between the incidence of loss making and the higher death rate of loss making firms in terms of explaining higher overall death rates seems to be fairly even. This is also apparent from Table 3.9, which presents probit estimates of entry into receivership in the two periods. The base group is firms with margins over 0.06 and lower margins are (0,1) dummies for margin below zero (loses), 0 to 3 per cent and 3 per cent to 6 per cent. Note that the base probability represented by the constant is almost identical in both specifications across the two periods. The probability of death is thus the same for the base group. The higher incidence of failure is, therefore, explained by the different distributions of firms across the profit categories and the higher death rate in the loss making zone. Firms with margins between 0 and 6 per cent had higher death rates in the early period, but they were not substantially higher or statistically significant. For loss making firms, the death rate was 25 points higher in the second period, without additional controls, and this failure rate was significant at the 10 per cent level.[23]

A more thorough exploration including other relevant factors suggests that two other key factors affecting failure rates are debt (which raises failure rates) and firm size (which lowers them). Sales growth prior to the period considered is the extra variable that differs across the time periods. Sales growth during the recession was not correlated with the incidence of failure, but sales growth prior to 1987 was weakly positively correlated with subsequent receivership. Table 3.10 shows that the base hazard of going

Table 3.10 Implied probabilities of company failure from regression in table 4.3 for the 1991–3 period

Representative firm	1988–99 Hazard	1991–3 Hazard
Operating profit margin >=.06	2.2	3.0
Operating profit margin >=.03 but <.06	3.3	3.7
Operating profit margin >=0 but <.03	4.0	4.0
Operating profit margin <0	13.1	16.6
Margin >=.06 and debt/assets=.42	5.8	4.8
Margin >=.06 and employees=164	4.5	4.0
Margin<0 & debt/assets=.42	17.6	25.4
Margin<0 & debt/assets=.42 & employees=164	23.0	30.1

Source: Taken from the second and fourth columns of Table 3.9; mean values were used for other characteristics not shown.

into receivership (evaluated at means but with margins above 6 per cent) was predicted to be 3 per cent in the recession. If the ratio of debt to assets was one standard deviation above the mean, this rose to 4.8 per cent; for a firm one standard deviation smaller than average, the failure rate was 4.2 per cent. A firm with margins between 3 per cent and 6 per cent had a failure rate of 3.7 per cent (it was 4 per cent if margins were between 0 and 3 per cent), whilst loss making firms had failure rates of 16.6 per cent. Being a loss making firm is, therefore, the crucial factor. A loss making firm with one standard deviation higher debt-asset ratio had a death rate of 25.4 per cent, and if it was also one deviation smaller than the average, this went up to 30 per cent. Again, the difference between pre and within recession characteristics is very important. Being a loss making firm in 1988–90 meant a 13.1 per cent likelihood of death, and this rose to 17.6 per cent if the firm had a one standard deviation higher debt–asset ratio, and 23 per cent if it was also one deviation smaller.[24]

Two additional observations are worth making. First, liquidation decisions are likely to reflect current expectations about the firm's future prospects in its markets, and, if the recession causes substantial revision of expectations downward, then this news will affect liquidation rates. Since the effects of the recession clearly vary by sector, at least some of these effects may be captured by industry dummies (industry details are not available for firms that exited prior to 1990 and so industry dummies can only be added for the later period). Second, past information on the duration of underperformance and its causes may be used to form expectations

Table 3.11 Probit estimates of firms going into receivership 1991–3

Going into receivership	1991–3
Profit margin <0 (t)	0.8562
	(0.1463)
Profit margin >=0 but <0.03 (t)	0.2702
	(0.2100)
Profit margin >=0.03 but <0.06 (t)	0.2815
	(0.1851)
Debt/assets (t)	0.9171
	(0.2593)
Cash/liabilities (t)	−0.2494
	(0.1989)
Ln employment (t)	−0.0855
	(0.0354)
Ln real sales(t)– Ln real sales(t-2)	−0.1040
	(0.1196)
Average margin 1982–99	−0.3385
	(0.4073)
Std. deviation of margin 1982–9	0.6087
	(0.6665)
2+ acquisitions 1986–90	0.2742
	(0.1294)
Constant	−1.102
	(0.3281)
Industry dummies	Yes
Sample size	1909
Pseudo R squared	0.1816
Log likelihood	−281.9

Note: Time t is 1991 and is lagged two years from this date. If 1991 was not available then 1990 was used instead.

about the future of each company. If the recession hit an otherwise successful firm unduly hard (perhaps because of temporary exposure through over rapid expansion), then this may be offset against current underperformance by those involved in the liquidation decision. As we discovered earlier, pre-recession growth, export intensity and company structure are all determinants of current vulnerability which might also affect current views of future performance.

These two observations suggests that it might be worth augmenting the regressions shown on Table 3.9, and Table 3.11 reports such a regression for 1991–3 including information not available for the 1988–90 period. The availability of this data restricts the sample size to just over 1900 firms with 92 failures. The correlation between debt measures within and before the recession is too high to reveal extra information. We capture pre-recession expansion by acquisition activity, and one digit industry dummies are included (and raise the explanatory power of the regression slightly). A pseudo R squared of 18 per cent is pretty good for equations such as this, and is in marked contrast to the vulnerability equations in Table 3.7 which were of the order of 4 per cent.[25] The industries with higher failure rates were miscellaneous private services, construction and, to a lesser degree, transport. As size and financial status of the firms involved are controlled for, this suggests that these industries went through a significant revision of expectations about future prospects as a result of the recession. The average of past performance and its variation were not well determined once current performance is controlled for (although the sign in both cases was consistent with those observed earlier explaining vulnerability). It seems reasonable to conclude from this that firms who underperformed prior to the recession were more likely to get into distress; however, once in trouble, past performance made little additional difference in predicting the likelihood that the firm went into receivership.

Selection: a summing up

In sum, only about 50 per cent of our sample thought themselves to have been badly affected by the recession. Since only 25 per cent of the firms in our sample took no action in response to recessionary pressures (see Chapter 4 below), it follows that many more firms reacted to recessionary pressures than absolutely had to. This suggests that some firms may have been more vulnerable to recessionary pressures than they were willing to admit. On the other hand, of the 50 per cent of the sample that were badly affected, only 5 per cent went into receivership and only 10 per cent were responsible for the bulk of sales, profits and employment loss. Since 20 per cent believed themselves to have been *'extremely severely'* affected, it follows that many more firms felt vulnerable to recessionary pressures than an outside observer might have thought. All of this means that determining what makes a firm *'vulnerable'* is a particularly hazardous undertaking.

This said, there is enough consistency in the results reported above with those in the previous section to suggest a basic continuum in the characteristics of survivors who were not badly affected by the recession, survivors who were *'extremely severely'* affected and firms that failed. Taking either of the last two types of firms as being *'vulnerable'*, it seems reasonable to associate enhanced vulnerability with small size and, more weakly, with faster pre-recession growth (particularly if it was acquisition led) and higher debt. These last two characteristics are liable to be associated with cash flow problems. It may also be the case that export oriented firms and subsidiaries of foreign firms are less vulnerable (at least they were less vulnerable in 1990) and that holding companies are more vulnerable, but these conclusions are sensitive to exactly how one defines 'vulnerable'. It is also clearly the case that pre-recession profitability is not a useful predictor of vulnerability and, indeed, all of the pre-recession characteristics of firms that we have examined together make an extremely unimpressive contribution to explaining the incidence of vulnerability across firms.

However, although it is hard to predict who gets into trouble during a recession in advance, one can get a pretty good idea which firms are going to go under once the recession has started, namely those firms which are badly hit at the onset of the recession. Firms which make operating losses at the start of a recession have a ticking clock counting down to failure. The clock ticks faster in a recession than in better trading conditions, it is faster for small firms, those with high levels of debt (especially if debt helped finance expansion through acquisition), and it is no slower if the firm had a good pre-recession performance record. Such a record does, however, mean that the firm is somewhat less likely to be observed in loss making territory in the first place.

Conclusions

There are (at least) seven stylised facts which might be used to summarise what we have discovered about company performance over the two most recent recessions in the UK:
- First, the dispersion in the performance of different firms has gradually increased over time, rising particularly noticeably in the two recessions covered by our data and never really returning to pre-recession levels.
- Second, the effects of recessions are highly skewed, with a relatively small number of firms suffering particularly badly.
- Third, while profits are highly persistent over time, the degree of persistence has been declining since the early 1970s. Further, the speed of the convergence of profits to a common norm seems to be a little slower in recessions than during booms.
- Fourth, the ranking of firms seems to be scrambled during recessions to a degree which does not occur in other periods. This said, the fact that low levels of profitability persist for long periods of time implies

that poor pre-recession performers will often be poor performers during recessions, but not as often as one might have expected. This means
that the increase in dispersion in company performance in recessions is
partly caused by poor pre-recession performers performing even more
poorly during the recession. This is not, however, the whole story, since
those firms who suffer a severe deterioration in performance during a
recession seem to be drawn from right across the distribution of firms.

- Fifth, there is no reason to think that some firms are more inherently
  vulnerable to recessions than others, nor that firms badly affected in one
  recession are unable to recover and prosper during a second recession
  which occurs ten years later.

- Sixth, while firms that get in trouble (for example make losses) are quite
  likely to fail, predicting which firm is likely to get in trouble is very hard.

- Seventh and finally, the difference between recessions in booms is not
  just that more firms get into trouble, but also that firms in trouble have
  a higher probability of failing. In a sense, there is a double hurdle
  facing firms threatened with extinction, and both hurdles rise in bad
  times.

These stylised facts enable us to hazard two broad generalisations about
the character of market selection processes. The first is that selection forces
have more diversity to work on in recessions than in booms, and, all things
being equal, this suggests that more industrial restructuring may take place
in recessions than typically occurs in booms. Second and rather more con-
troversially, it is not the case that persistently poorly performing firms are
the only firms who suffer during recessions. Rather, recession induced selection pressures seem also to single a surprisingly large number of firms
whose pre-recession performance was not at the bottom end of the distribution. This, in turn, begs the question of what criteria are used by the
selection pressures which are unleashed in recessions. Here the data seem
to be much less clear. The simple fact is that it is relatively difficult to ascertain exactly what criteria are used to discriminate between firms,
regardless of whether the vulnerability of firms to recessionary pressures
is measured by subjective measures of well being or failure. It is certainly
the case that pre-recession profitability provides only a poor guide to within
recession performance, and, in fact, firm size is probably the most robust
predictor of vulnerability in our data (although it does not take us very far).
In fact, we are more likely to spot a vulnerable firm by looking at how well
it performs at the beginning of a recession than at how it performed prior
to the recession.

As we noted earlier, nothing that we have done in this chapter enables
us to say anything rigorously persuasive on the question of whether the

market selection mechanisms unleashed in recessions are efficient or inefficient. However, having sifted through the data, we have formed the impression that market selection criteria may be rather myopic. The two pieces of evidence which point in this direction are the fact that many of the firms who suffered badly in the recession prospered prior to it and firms that grew rapidly prior to the recession, particularly those who were very acquisition orientated and ran up high levels of debt, proved to be rather vulnerable to the collapse in demand which heralded the advent of the 1991 slump. Although it is possible that high levels of accounting profits and high pre-recession growth rates can occasionally mask a genuinely failing firm, it is hard to believe that this is typically the case. This means that at least some fundamentally sound firms who happen to fall into transitory difficulties are selected against when times get rough, and either are forced to exit or to drastically alter their operations when this may not be really necessary. For these firms, recessionary pressures are more a matter of bad timing than anything else, and the actions they are forced to take should rightfully be considered as part of the costs of the recession. Quite how large one thinks these additional costs of recessions really are also depends on whether one believes that the apparently large random element in market selection which we have observed in our data reflects the weakness of our data or a genuine randomness in the operation of market selection forces. None of these considerations necessarily means that the selection induced changes which occur in recessions are not, on balance, productive. They do, however, suggest that the net gains which they create might more modest than appears at first sight.

One final observation is worth making. The data suggest that the effects of recessions are very selective, affecting a relatively small number of firms very severely but only moderately affected many others. As we have seen, predicting who these 'extremely severely' affected are is very difficult since some firms in badly affected industries prosper in recessions, while others in growing sectors suffer (the same applies to failed firms). This selectivity is reflected in the very uneven generation of job destruction across firms, with a small number of firms accounting for most job losses, often through plant closure. As others have noted, this data is inconsistent with the view that *aggregate* shocks, which have widespread and broadly similar effects across firms, are the main cause of recessionary pressures.[26] Interest rate movements and credit restrictions are often cited as examples of aggregate shocks, but a moment's reflection suggests that they are unlikely to have similar effects on all firms. As we saw in Chapter 2, most firms in our sample believed that a decline in domestic demand was the source of most of their problems. However, even if all consumers suffered exactly the same erosion in earnings, a decline in demand is likely to have different effects in different sectors (how different depends on the income elasticity of demand) and, depending on the degree of market fragmentation, within sectors. Some have referred to these idiosyncratic shocks as *allocative*, and see them as calling for reorganisations of factor inputs.[27] Regardless of whether it is idiosyncrasies in shocks or differences in firms' abilities which accounts for the selectivity in the effects of recessionary pressures which we have observed, the simple fact is that describing what happens during recessions using simple macroeconomic aggregates and representative firm models of the economy produces a seriously distorted picture of events. Recessions are about what happens to differences between firms much more than they are about what happens to firms on average.

4 Changes in corporate strategy and structure

Introduction

To understand how a firm responds to market pressures, one must know something about the relative costs and benefits associated with the different options open to it. These, in turn, depend on many things, including current market conditions and current expectations of future market conditions. The costs and benefits of different actions also depend on what the firm is good at; that is on its core skills or capabilities. Indeed, not only are the *core competences* of a corporation likely to profoundly affect how it responds to shocks, they are also likely to play an important role in affecting how severely any given shock will affect the firm. Able firms may need to respond less to environmental change and, when they do respond, may well do so in quite different ways from less able firms.

The difficulty with this line of argument—and indeed with the huge business strategy literature that has grown up around the so-called 'resource based theory of the firm'—is that it is very difficult to identify and measure a firm's capabilities. While one would, in principle, like to examine the link between particular skills or competences and the incidence of particular actions taken by firms, this is beyond our reach here. What we can do, however, is to explore two more modest propositions. The first is the proposition that firms interested in maximising profits are likely to take any action which improves their profitability. Since it is not at all obvious that any particular response (cutting costs, restructuring debt, raising prices, and so on) is likely to be better than any other in all circumstances, it seems reasonable to expect that firms that do respond to the recession will use many instruments, and that the mix of instruments used will not be the same for all firms.

Of course, some firms are likely to respond differently from others, and the second proposition that we can explore is that the capabilities of large firms (to choose the most easy to observe difference between firms) differ

71

from those of small firms and, as a consequence, they respond differently to recessionary pressures. There are two strands to this argument. The first starts with the observation that, to develop many core capabilities, firms must make substantial investments in fixed costs which are also sunk. Large, diversified firms can spread these costs over more activities which operate on a larger scale, they may also be better placed to absorb the risks associated with such investments and they may find it easier to finance them.[1] Such arguments apply particularly well to investments in activities like advertising and R&D, leaving one with at least a weak presumption that large firms may feel less pressure to respond to recessionary pressures and, when they do respond, they may focus less on costs and more on product differentiation. The second strand of argument cuts the other way. However rich in resources and capabilities a large firm may be, the simple fact is that acting coherently is more difficult the larger and more diverse a firm is. What is more, the ability to anticipate adverse shocks and understand where they come from lessens as the firm's own operations become more complex. Needless to say, these problems are not a function of firm size alone. Firms with tighter governance structures and tighter internal control systems are likely to be more able to adapt to shocks than others. The implications of this second argument is that any link that we observe between firm size on the one hand, and the incidence and type of response a firm makes on the other, is likely to be conditioned on how well firms are run. Firms with loose ownership and/or internal structures are likely to face more problems, and respond less effectively to them.

However firms respond to recessionary pressures, it seems reasonable to believe that the consequence will be changes in how they operate and in the markets where they compete. Indeed, some people believe that the pace of structural change accelerates in recessions, and that these changes fuel much of the pro-cyclical burst of productivity growth that we typically observe. At its broadest level, this is the theme that we will address in this chapter, and the plan is as follows. We start in the following section by looking at the strategic, financial and cost control oriented responses made by firms to recessionary pressures, distinguishing between those firms who were *'extremely severely'* affected by the recession and all others. Next, we focus on investment behaviour, and chart the extent to which firms abandon or postpone investments in physical, human, technological and marketing capital. This exercise is pursued further in the fourth section where we look at the relationship between a number of observable characteristics of firms (such as size, type of organisational structure, ownership structure, recent performance and so on), and the kinds of decisions that they made during the recession.

Strategic responses to the recession

Recessionary pressures typically manifest themselves through a sharp drop in demand. For firms with high fixed costs and zero marginal costs, the whole of the corresponding decline in revenue goes straight to the bottom line and lowers profits directly. When marginal costs are non-zero, reductions in output rates and, perhaps, a change in price can be used to modify the effect that the adverse shift in demand has on profits, and there are a range of marketing and cost cutting initiatives open to most firms which can be used to cushion further the blow on profits. It is clear that profit maximising firms will take *all* of the actions which are necessary to restore their fortunes; that is, they will cut costs, change prices and production levels, financially reengineer themselves as necessary and so on. Absent any unusual cost or benefit associated with any one particular type of strategic response, it is hard to see why firms might choose only one type of action (like cutting costs, altering their debt structure, and so on). It follows that one expects to observe a wide range of responses to recessionary pressure by any particular firm, and across all firms.[2]

This is not, however, an uncontroversial proposition. It has often been argued that there are at least two generic (that is mutually exclusive) strategy options which managers must make a choice between: cost leadership and product differentiation.[3] The argument turns on the observation that cost leadership often means exploiting scale economies or learning effects— something that requires product standardisation (or at least limits the degree to which a firm can customise or differentiate its product). Differentiators, by contrast, need to segment markets and customise their products. More subtly, the process engineering, upstream focus of cost leaders sits awkwardly with the new product, downstream focus of differentiators, and it is hard to believe that many firms will be able to sustain both. If these conjectures are correct, we expect to see firms focusing either on cutting costs or on repositioning their product and/or creating new markets in response to recessionary pressures, but not both.

As it happens, the data are strongly inconsistent with the hypothesis that firms do not confine their responses to recessionary pressures to particular types of strategies. Table 4.1 shows the answers to a question which we asked about how firms had responded to the recession. Firms were offered a range of (non-exclusive) choices grouped into three broad categories: *'financial decisions'*, *'strategic decisions'*, and *'cost control'*, and they were asked to identify those which were *'very important'*, those that were *'taken and of some importance'* (not shown on the table) and those *'actions not taken'*. The first two columns of the table show the percentage of *all* firms

Table 4.1 Responses to the recession

'Which of the following actions were taken in response to the problems your company has faced in the recession, and how important have they been in overcoming these problems?'

	% all firms		% 'extremely severely' affected	
	'Action very important'	'Action not taken'	'Action very important'	'Action not taken'
Financial decisions				
Disposal of assets	25	42	50	19
Reduce dividend cover	11	54	26	22
Introduce a rights issue	10	75	14	77
Reschedule debt	10	67	21	55
Increase short term borrowing	11	56	25	43
Strategic decisions				
Focus on core businesses	54	13	64	5
Increase prices	9	48	13	66
Change marketing strategies	25	23	26	13
Merge with/acquire another company	10	69	8	73
Rationalise product lines	15	39	15	33
Develop overseas markets	23	37	12	50
Cost Control				
Close establishments	30	40	57	21
Reduce employment	49	13	82	1
Reduce employee wage growth	39	11	67	2
Reduce inventories	32	25	55	19
Scrap outdated machinery	8	57	11	57
Reduce headquarters costs	31	23	52	8
Contract out auxiliary services	6	56	7	45

who thought that each specific action was '*very important*' or '*not taken*'; the analogous percentages are shown in the third and fourth columns for firms who identified themselves as being '*extremely severely affected*' by the recession.

Although many actions were cited by firms as being '*very important*' and many firms identified more than one action as being '*very important*', the first feature of Table 4.1 worth noting is that 107 firms stated that no action was taken in any of the areas listed on the table. This is, of course, a reflection of the fact that the effects of the recession were very unevenly felt across the population of firms (only 4 of these 107 firms described themselves as being 'extremely severely' affected). Further, an additional 21 firms cited only 'focus on core business', a strategy (or set of buzz words) which captured the imagination of managers long before the onset of the recession and may not, therefore, be truly a response to current recessionary pressures. Adding these to the non-responders gives an upper bound estimate of the non-response rate of 22 per cent of the 586 core respondents; that is about one in five firms did not respond to recessionary pressures in any of the 18 ways suggested on the table (except 'focus') or suggest any alternative response not suggested.

The second interesting feature of the table is that most of the firms who responded to recessionary pressures concentrated on controlling costs. Indeed, 378 firms (65 per cent of the core sample) cited at least one cost control factor as being 'very important'; that is, most of the firms in the sample who took an action in response to the recession did so (at least) with the intention of controlling costs. Relatively few firms cited any of the individual 'financial decisions' as being very important, and, with the exception of 'focus on core business' (cited by 318 firms), relatively few firms cited any of the individual 'strategic decisions' as being very important. In fact, with the clear exception of 'focus on core business' and the marginal exception of 'change marketing strategies', many more firms cited 'action not taken' than 'action very important' with respect to the various financial and strategic decisions listed on the table. By contrast, nearly half the firms in the sample regarded reducing employment as very important and a solid 30 per cent plus cited closing establishments, reducing employee wage growth, reducing inventories and reducing headquarters costs as being very important. Further, with the exception of closing establishments, many more firms thought that these actions were 'very important' than decided that no action was appropriate.

The third interesting feature of Table 4.1 is the things that firms did not do in response to the recession. Only a very small minority of firms (about 10 per cent of the full sample) regarded reducing dividends, selling equity, rescheduling debt or increasing short term debt as being 'very important' (or even 'of some importance'), and a clear majority of firms took none of these actions. Even 'extremely severely' affected firms were more likely not to take these actions than to regard them as 'very important' or 'of some importance' (the exception to this was reducing dividend cover). Similarly, relatively few firms ('extremely severely' affected or not) regarded increasing prices, changing marketing strategies, rationalising product lines or developing overseas markets as being 'very important' or even 'of some *importance*', and most took no action in any of these areas. The exception was changing marketing strategies, which seems to have occurred fairly widely despite the fact that relatively few firms thought that it was very important. Very few firms regarded capital scrapping as being either '*very important*' or '*of some importance*' (the same applied to contracting out auxiliary services).

The third and fourth column of Table 4.1 concentrates only on firms who were '*extremely severely*' affected by the recession. Almost all of these firms responded to recessionary pressures, and most disposed of assets, closed establishments, and reduced employment, wage growth, inventories and headquarters costs. Many fewer of them reduced dividends than reduced wages growth or employment. The tendency for distressed firms to focus on costs in response to recessionary pressures was, if anything, more marked than that shown by the full sample of firms: 91 per cent of firms who were '*extremely severely*' affected by the recession made a '*cost control*' response, while fewer than 40 per cent of those firms who were less severely affected made such a response. Only 19 per cent of the firms who cited at least one '*strategic decision*' as being very important were '*extremely severely*' affected by the recession. '*Focus on core business*' was (by far) the most important strategic decision made by firms in our sample (only 77 firms thought that it was '*not important*'), but many firms who were not '*extremely severely*' affected by the recession viewed it as an important action to take.

The eighteen different responses listed on Table 4.1 are neither exhaustive nor mutually exclusive, and many firms took several actions simultaneously. Most of the correlations among the choices made by firms are related to focus and closure/cost control strategies: 82 per cent of the firms who disposed of assets also cited '*focus on core businesses*', 62 per cent of them closed plants, 70 per cent reduced employment and more than 50 per cent of them reduced headquarters costs, inventories and employee wage growth. 76 per cent of those who closed establishments also increased their focus on core business, 85 per cent reduced employee wage growth, and more than 55 per cent of them reduced headquarters costs and inventories. Many firms that embarked on closure strategies seemed to equate them with focus strategies: just under 50 per cent of the firms who thought that '*focus on core business*' was important closed establishments or reduced wage growth, headquarters costs or inventories, while 61 per cent of them reduced employment. Needless to say, those firms who were '*extremely severely*' affected by the recession were particularly prone to equate focus strategies with plant closure and employment reduction.

In short, although only one in five respondents to our survey admitted to being *'extremely severely'* affected by the recession, nearly two thirds of them cited cost control as being a *'very important'* response. Hard hit firms made a wider set of responses than others, but nearly two thirds of the firms who responded to the survey tried to cut costs. In practice, cutting costs meant closing plants, reducing wages growth and shedding labour, something that many firms described as *'increasing focus'* despite the fact that few of them rationalised their product lines. What is most interesting and surprising is that relatively few firms reduced dividends, contracted out auxiliary services, scrapped capital or developed new overseas markets.

It is useful to put these results into perspective by drawing on the analogy to be made between the effects of new entry competition and the effects of a recession on incumbent firms in a market. In both cases, the (residual) demand facing particular firms shifts in (due to increases in market supply and decreases in market demand respectively), often to such an extent that some sort of remedial action is called for. Since both causes have a similar apparent effect on the market position of firms, it is reasonable to surmise that both might elicit similar responses. In fact, although the answer is not entirely clear, it seems to be the case that this inference is wrong.

Several questionnaire surveys have examined how firms respond to new entry competition and two points of comparison with the results discussed above are worth noting.[4] First, as with responses to the recession, many incumbent firms (often 40–50 per cent of the samples being examined) facing entry threats reveal themselves to be extremely selective in their response to new entry competition. Although more firms seem to have responded to the recession than typically report themselves as responding to entry, this is probably due to the severity of the most recent UK recession on the one hand, and the relatively weak competitive threat posed by many new entrants in their early years of operation on the other. Second and more interesting is the fact that responses to entry tend to be dominated by the use of marketing strategies (but not prices) to block or retard the rate of entry, rather than by the use of cost control to modify its effects on the (incumbent) firm. It is, of course, possible that this result is an artifact of how the entry questionnaires were constructed (most of them focused on strategic actions like *'increase advertising'*, *'use idle capacity to deter entry'*, *'limit price'*, and so on, and they offered respondents very few cost control options), and there are numerous case studies which feature cost cutting responses to entry.[5] Nevertheless, this difference in questionnaire results between the two types of study is not inconsistent with the view that firms feel unable to modify the effects of major shocks like recessions on the demand for their products, however confident they are of coping with changes in the demand for their products induced by changes in competition.

Table 4.2 Redeployment and redundancy

'*Did your company use any of the following methods of workforce alteration in any establishment that continued in operation in the period 1990–92?*'

	% all firms		
	Yes	No	Most widely used
Redeployment between job functions	72	19	13
Recruitment freeze/natural wastage	77	14	21
Early retirement	53	34	10
Voluntary redundancy	45	43	14
Compulsory redundancy	72	21	42
	% 'extremely severely' affected		
	Yes	No	Most widely used
Redeployment between job functions	71	14	4
Recruitment freeze/natural wastage	88	5	19
Early retirement	61	24	2
Voluntary redundancy	46	38	7
Compulsory redundancy	90	5	67

It is evident that a major component of the cost reduction strategy that most firms chose to follow was reducing labour costs, and Tables 4.2 and 4.3 provide some information on how this was done by the companies who responded to our survey. Nearly three quarters of the firms in the sample redeployed workers, froze recruitment and made compulsory redundancies (only 49 firms used none of the five methods of workforce alteration listed on the table), and 40 per cent of the sample reported that compulsory redundancy was the most widely used method of slimming employed by them. The consequence of this is that the 556 firms who answered our survey and had complete company accounts reduced their combined employment from 3.08 million in 1989 to 2.95 million in 1992 (about 4 per cent). Firms who were '*extremely severely*' affected typically contracted by 22 per cent (the median) and those '*severely*' affected by 7 per cent. Those less affected by the recession showed modest net job growth (see also Table 3.5). Although virtually all of the job losses occurred among firms '*severely*' or '*extremely severely*' affected, the firms in our sample that were '*extremely severely*' affected were, on the whole, small and, as a consequence, they were not responsible for a huge proportion of all jobs lost.

Table 4.3 Distribution of percentage changes in employment across boom and recession periods

	Less than ˉ15	ˉ15–ˉ11	ˉ10–ˉ6	ˉ5–ˉ2	ˉ1–0	0–⁺1	⁺2–⁺5	⁺6–⁺10	⁺10–⁺15	⁺15 or more
1992–1989										
Number of firms	5	6	5	38	257	211	29	3	0	4
Total change in bond	ˉ150	ˉ79	ˉ35	ˉ81	ˉ52	+40	+56	+22	–	+150
1989–1986										
Number of firms	2	3	4	19	109	323	55	5	6	6
Total change in bond	ˉ116	ˉ40	ˉ28	ˉ35	ˉ20	+71	+118	+39	+79	+198
Difference in employment change for bond across two periods	ˉ35	ˉ39	ˉ7	ˉ46	ˉ32	ˉ31	ˉ62	ˉ17	ˉ79	ˉ48

As the bottom panel of Table 4.2 shows, for a clear two thirds majority of these distressed firms, compulsory redundancy was the most important method of job shedding (just over 90 per cent resorted to compulsory redundancies one way or the other).

As we noted earlier (in Chapter 3), job losses are highly concentrated in a relatively small number of firms, but it is worth noting that job gains during booms are also highly concentrated.[6] Between 1989 and 1992, 311 of the responding 556 firms with complete accounts data shed employment (only 56 per cent). These contracting firms shed 391,000 jobs, whereas expanding ones added 268,000. In the boom years 1986–9, 74 per cent firms (395 out of 532) expanded employment, adding 506,000 jobs (contracting ones lost 239,000). However, the biggest employment changes often reflect acquisition and divestment rather than organic growth, particularly in the boom years when acquisitional activity was high. Between 1989 and 1992, the two biggest losers shed nearly 100,000 jobs and the two biggest expanders on the same period added 110,000 jobs. Table 4.3 shows how the distribution of firm employment expansion and contraction varied across firms in boom and recession conditions. Both expansion and contraction were dominated by a few firms who made large employment changes, while the bulk of firms shifted from being small growers (less

Table 4.4 *Wage freezes*

'In the period 1990–91, did your company operate, at any time, a temporary
'wage freeze' covering a substantial part of the workforce?'

per cent

Wage freeze duration	Companies who operated a freeze	'extremely severely' affected companies who operated a freeze
Not introduced	48.3	15.4
3 months or less	2.7	4.8
4 to 6 months	9.9	5.8
7 to 12 months	17.1	16.4
More than 12 months	19.0	52.9

than 1,000 job gains) to small losers (less than 1,000 job losses) when the
economy moved from boom to recession. Between 1989 and 1992, 16 firms
shed more than 5,000 employees and accounted for over 260,000 job losses.
Between 1986–9, 9 firms shed more than 5,000 jobs, accounting for
180,000 job losses. The number of firms shedding up to 1,000 jobs rose
from 109 in the boom period to 257 in the recession, but the difference
amounted to only 32,000 net job losses between the two periods. A similar story applies to the declining number of rapid growers. In short, job
shedding is heavily concentrated on recession years but not obviously more
concentrated than job growth in booms.[7]

Reducing labour costs can also involve cutting wages. This usually did
not take the form of a cut in nominal wages but, rather, occurred through
some form of wage freeze. Given that the annual rate of inflation over the
recession period 1990–93 was about 4.5 per cent, a wage freeze initiated
at the beginning of the recession (in 1990) and maintained to 1993
amounted to a modest real wage cut. Table 4.4 shows the incidence and
duration of wage freezes for all firms, and for those who were 'extremely
severely' affected by the recession. Only 285 firms in the core sample introduced a wage freeze (including 75 per cent of the 'extremely severely'
affected firms). Although it is almost certain that all of the firms in our
sample made many efforts to control wages and salaries growth, the fact
is that many more of them seem to have adjusted quantities than prices in
their attempts to control their wage bill. In addition, the scale of price adjustment which they managed appears to be rather modest relative to the
employment changes noted above.[8]

A clear majority of the firms who responded to our survey thought that
'focus on core business' was very important (only 13 per cent of the respond-

Table 4.5 *Downsizing*
*'In the period 1990–92 did your company engage in any of the following
actions concerning the size of its operations?'*

	% all firms	% 'extremely severely' affected
Sell any part of its operation to another company(ies)?	35	59
Have a management buyout of any part of its operation?	15	20
Contract out to another company functions or services previously undertaken within company?	25	30
Close one or more establishments?	50	64

ents did not), and the extensive use of plant closure and asset disposal by
responding firms seems to be consistent with realising this goal. There are,
of course, other ways for a firm to concentrate its activities on core businesses. The 1980s saw an increased use of management buyouts and a
number of firms began to contract out some of their non-peripheral activities to specialists. To ascertain how frequently firms used these different
methods of slimming or focusing, we asked companies to describe the actions that they took in adjusting the size and scope of their activities to suit
the circumstances which they found themselves in. As Table 4.5 shows, 51
per cent of all firms in the sample (and 65 per cent of those who were *'extremely severely'* affected by the recession) closed one or more establishments,
while 36 per cent (nearly 42 per cent of those *'extremely severely'* affected)
sold off part of their operations and less than a quarter initiated a MBO. More
than two thirds of the 218 firms who sold part of their operations also closed
one or more establishments, but fewer than a third of sellers initiated an MBO.
Contracting out or initiating a management buyout were evidentially not
widely used by the vast majority of firms in our sample. Most firms just simply closed the plants that they could not sell to outside buyers.

These results are not terribly difficult to understand. Management
buyouts generally involve shouldering large debt, a policy which has relatively little appeal during a severe recession. Contracting out has been
widely discussed in the UK, but most of the major initiatives have come
from the public sector, and it is not clear that contracting out has been as
widely used by private sector organisations. Firms that are sympathetic to
the notion of substituting markets for hierarchies seem to be more inclined
to try to use market-like incentives internally (for example by creating profit

centres around specific activities, and having them bid for funds from the corporate parent) than they are to use external markets to purchase particular services. The one set of markets which corporate managers do frequently have recourse to is the capital market, and our data does suggest that the relatively high level of reshuffling of corporate assets through divestiture which developed throughout the 1980s continued into the recession. At the end of the day, however, plant closure was easily the most common form of slimming undertaken by firms. This may reflect relatively low resale values associated with sunk assets or depressed prices during the recession. It may also be the natural form which capital scrapping takes in highly integrated plants. Individual pieces of capital equipment used in stand alone tasks can be scrapped and replaced wherever they are found in a plant, but the many machine tools linked together in an integrated assembly line stand or fall together. Hence, major retooling operations can be easier to manage by closing, and then rebuilding, a plant than by implementing a series of incremental changes applied to one machine at a time.[9]

In short, most responses made by firms to the recession seem to be aimed at controlling costs. Very few firms considered pricing or marketing strategy responses to be very important, and relatively few tried to rationalise product lines or develop overseas markets. With the exception of disposing of assets, only a very small number of firms contemplated major financial re-engineering exercises in the face of the recession: only a few firms chose to reduce dividend cover, increase short-term borrowing or reschedule debt. The conclusion that firms focus on cost is slightly clouded by the fact that a clear majority of the firms responding to our survey cited *'focus on core business'* as an important strategic decision. A closer inspection of the data suggests that for many firms focus strategies are effectively about closing plants and reducing employment. As one might expect, most of those firms who reported themselves to be *'extremely severely'* affected by the recession were particularly likely to translate *'focus'* into *'closure'*, and they shed jobs primarily through compulsory redundancies. The total number of jobs shed in our sample was heavily concentrated in about 54 firms, a somewhat larger number of big job sheds than in the previous boom. Nearly half the firms in our sample introduced a wage freeze, including most of the firms who were *'extremely severely'* affected by the recession (their freezes were longer).

Reorganisations and investment behaviour

Investment behaviour is almost always substantially disrupted during a recession and, indeed, one of the most recognisable features of the business cycle is the wide fluctuation in plant and equipment expenditures which occurs as the economy moves from boom to slump. Some economists and popular commentators have speculated that investment in a range of intangibles like training, R&D and marketing is also likely to be adversely affected during recessions. This hypothesis is based on the notion that firms will be anxious to reduce their fixed costs when demand falls, and that many of them will have trouble in financing sunk investment expenditures in intangible capital during a slump. Further, stocks of intangibles are notoriously difficult to measure, and the benefits they produce may be easy for myopic managers to underestimate. This view is not, however, universally held. The 'pit stop' theory of recessions suggests that investments which are management time intensive may be delayed until periods of low demand. Such investments, sometimes referred to as investments in organisational capital, may induce countercyclical variations in investments in training and, perhaps, in product or process innovation and marketing. That is, many firms may bring forward investment in intangibles at the same time as they cut investment in plant and equipment.

To explore these ideas, we examined a wide range of activities undertaken by firms to adapt their activities to current market conditions. We started by examining investments in organisational structure. If there is any substance to the theory that firms invest in organisational capital during recessions, then it should be observable in the ways they reorganise themselves during recessions. We then moved on to look at the timing of investment decisions, and compared decisions about investing in tangibles like plant and equipment with decisions about investing in intangibles like R&D and training. Finally, we looked at the consequences of all of these decisions on the product portfolio that firms bring to the market.

We first asked firms to identify their organisational structure using the characterisation discussed in Chapter 2 and reproduced for convenience as Figure 4.1 here. The question immediately following asked firms if their organisational structure had changed since 1985 and, if so, to identify the primary reason for change. The responses that we received are displayed in Table 4.6. The most surprising feature of the table is that only 32 per cent of the sample reported no change in their organisational structure over the eight years covered by the question.[10] Changes seem to have occurred both before and during the recession. Many of the firms who made changes to their organisational structure in response to merger (21 per cent in total) or an expansion of their company (22 per cent) presumably did so prior to the recession, while most of those who made changes due to the recession or contractions in firm size (21 per cent) presumably did so after the

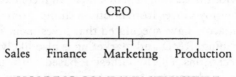

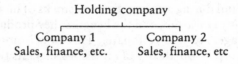

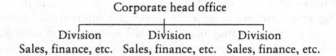

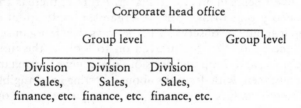

Figure 4.1 *Stylised company structures*

onset of the recession. Sixteen per cent of the changes in organisational structure were timed with the arrival of a new Chief Executive Officer (CEO), a figure that is hard to interpret because many firms use new CEOs as change agents brought in to deal with problems created by merger or by the recession.[11] '*Extremely severely*' affected firms were as likely to make a change induced by merger as all firms in the sample were, but were more than twice as likely to make an organisational change in response to a contraction of the company or the recession. They were (surprisingly) less likely to attribute the cause of change to a new CEO.[12]

The 1980s saw a major wave of merger and take-over activity which reduced the degree of diversification (and the number of conglomerates)

Table 4.6 *Changes in organizational structure*
'If your company's organisational structure has changed since 1985 what was the primary reason for the change?'

	% all firms	% 'extremely severely' affected firms
Merger or takeover of another company	21	20
Potential hostile takeover by another company	1	1
New Chief Executive Officer	16	12
Expansion of company	22	14
Contraction of company	8	17
Reorganisation induced by recession	13	27
Other reasons	16	11
No change	32	32

built up through the sustained period of merger activity which took place in the 1960s and 1970s.[13] Since many of the mergers and takeovers which took place in the 1980s were designed to increase corporate focus, one would have expected such trends to continue unabated during the recession. However, 43 per cent of the sample reorganised because of merger or expansion while only 21 per cent because of contraction or recession. Although it is very speculative, this might be taken to suggest that recent trends in corporate reorganisation actually slowed down during the recession and, therefore, that recessions are not necessarily the phase of the business cycle when organisational change is at its maximum. What seems to be more clear than how the incidence of change varies over the cycle is how its character changes. Fifty-two per cent of the firms who changed their organisational structure because of contraction or the recession sold off plants and 70 per cent closed plants (34 per cent did both). However, only 41 per cent of the firms who changed their organisational structure because of merger or expansion also sold off plants, and only 48 per cent closed plants (23 per cent did both). These figures suggest not so much a change in the trend towards increased corporate focus during the recession as a shift in the manner in which it was being accomplished. That is, *'increasing corporate focus'* in the middle 1980s usually meant buying and selling operations to achieve a better balanced or more logical portfolio of businesses, while in the early 1990s it often meant closing establishments.

We also asked firms whether they made changes in their: *management methods, production processes, labour organisation,* and *wage payment systems* and, if so, whether these changes were induced by the recession.

Four hundred and one firms (nearly 70 per cent of the sample) changed their management methods, but only 27 per cent of these changes were induced by the recession. Changes in labour organisation were also very frequent (67 per cent firms made them), and were much more likely to be made in response to the recession (54 per cent of them were). Changes in production processes and in wage payment systems were relatively infrequent (only 258 and 255 occurred respectively), and they were generally not induced by the recession (only 22 per cent and 36 per cent were respectively).[14]

Thus, although firms seem to change their organisational structures very regularly, mergers or expansion of the firms were about twice as likely to induce a restructuring than contraction of the firm or recessionary pressures. Of the more modest changes in systems and processes we observed, only changes in labour organisation were more likely to be induced by the recession as not. If it is truly the case that the opportunity costs of change fall sharply in recessions, these results suggest that other costs of change seem to rise in recessions and are of sufficient importance to inhibit what might otherwise be a countercyclical variation in organisational restructuring.

The second question that we asked about investment behaviour focused on whether certain types of investment in intangibles were brought forward by firms during the recession. Table 4.7 displays the responses that we received. As one might expect, the most common changes in investment plans were to postpone or abandon investments in plant/machinery. In general, three times as many firms postponed or abandoned major investments as brought them forward. Planned investments in buildings were also severely cut back by just under half the sample. However, less than a third of the sample cut back on marketing expenditures or investment in training, and less than a fifth postponed or abandoned planned investments in R&D, product innovation and process innovation.

Of course, investment activity does not cease in a recession, and not all projects are abandoned or postponed. Thus, while only one in seven firms actually brought forward planned investments in plant/machinery and fewer than one in ten brought forward investments in buildings, nearly a third brought forward training expenditures and new product innovations, a quarter brought forward new process innovations and marketing expenditures, and just under a fifth brought forward investments in R&D. Two hundred and thirty-six firms brought forward either product or process innovations, and 108 of them also brought forward R&D expenditures. Many of these innovators brought forward training plans and marketing expenditures as well (118 and 81 firms respectively), but only 54 brought forward expenditures on plant/machinery (127 postponed or abandoned

Table 4.7 *Investment in tangibles and intangibles*
'Please indicate if your company abandoned, postponed or brought forward
any of the following types of investment plans in the period 1990–92'

	% all firms		
	Abandoned	Postponed	Brought forward
Investment in plant/machinery	6	41	14
Investment in buildings	14	28	10
Investment in R&D	5	15	20
New product innovation	2	9	34
New process innovation	3	10	26
Training staff members	4	24	31
Advertising/marketing expenditure	7	26	23
	% 'extremely severely' affected firms		
	Abandoned	Postponed	Brought forward
Investment in plant/machinery	15	50	11
Investment in buildings	27	25	4
Investment in R&D	15	18	8
New product innovation	5	12	30
New process innovation	6	13	19
Training staff members	7	34	20
Advertising/marketing expenditure	14	37	20

plans to invest in plant/machinery). Amongst other things, this suggests
either that investments in these types of intangible capital are less complementary than is frequently believed, or that the investments in intangible
human, technological and marketing capital which occur during recessions
are qualitatively different from those which occur at other stages of the business cycle (we will return to these issues in Chapter 6 below).

Finally, as the bottom part of Table 4.7 shows, firms who were '*extremely
severely*' affected by the recession were more likely to abandon than postpone all types of investments, and were less likely to bring investment
expenditures of any type forward (with the exception of new product innovations). In particular, 65 per cent of those who were '*extremely severely*'
affected postponed or abandoned plant/machinery investments (only 10 per
cent brought them forward), while 31 per cent of those who were '*moderately*' or '*not at all*' affected postponed or abandoned plant/machinery
investments (19 per cent brought them forward). This said, these firms do

Table 4.8 Investment behaviour and the expected duration of the recession

	% firms who abandoned or postponed investments, and thought that:		
	the recession was over	the recession would last ≤ 1 year	the recession would last > 1 year
Investment in plant/machinery	26	47	51
Investment in buildings	20	38	49
Investment in R&D	9	20	23
New product innovation	4	10	13
New process innovation	11	11	15
Training staff members	22	27	30
Advertising/marketing expenditure	35	32	3

	% firms who brought forward investments, and thought that:		
	the recession was over	the recession would last ≤ 1 year	the recession would last > 1 year
Investment in plant/machinery	29	11	14
Investment in buildings	38	7	8
Investment in R&D	33	21	17
New product innovation	38	33	35
New process innovation	27	28	26
Training staff members	44	29	31
Advertising/marketing expenditure	24	21	25

not appear to have cut investments in intangible capital proportionately harder than they cut investments in plant/machinery.[15]

'*Animal spirits*' often feature as part of many explanations about the volatility of investment behaviour during recessions. Although our data do not provide much information on this, some clues can be gleaned from Table 4.8 which shows how decisions about investment were related to expectations about the length of the recession. As one might imagine, firms who thought (in the Spring of 1993) that the recession would last longer than a year were much more likely to abandon all forms of investment, although this tendency is more marked for investment in plant and machinery than for advertising or training. Conversely, those who thought that the recession was over were much more likely to bring forward investment in plant and machinery. More interesting is a second observation, namely that decisions about investments in plant and machinery, buildings and R&D seem to be far more sensitive to expectations about the duration of the recession than the other four forms of investment shown on the table.

This data is not consistent with the view that investments in intangibles like physical, human, technological and marketing goodwill capital are particularly severely affected by recessionary pressures, or recession induced fluctuations in animal spirits. While they are almost certainly sunk and add to a firm's fixed costs, investments in intangibles like R&D, training and marketing are rarely as expensive or cash-intensive as investments in plant/ machinery or buildings. Further, they often require complementary labour inputs whose opportunity cost is lower when labour is underutilised (this is particularly true for expenditures on training).[16] Certainly, new processes (and, less clearly, products) often involve new working routines that may be easier and less costly to introduce in recessions. Although it would clearly be difficult to sustain the view that total investment (investment in plant plus investment in intangibles) does not fall in recessions, it does seem to be the case that the fall-off in total investment is less than the fall off in investment in plant and that, as a consequence, the ratio of investment in intangibles to investment in plant moves counter cyclically.

Sooner or later, investments in organisational structure or in certain kinds of knowledge result in some changes in a firm's market operations. Although it is clear that most of the immediate responses to the recession made by firms are concentrated on cutting costs and rationalising the range of businesses undertaken by the firm, a surprisingly large number of firms brought forward new product innovations. Table 4.9 shows the net effect of these changes on the product range offered to the market by each firm. A total of 469 firms (including 74 who were 'extremely severely' affected by the recession) introduced new product lines or services to either existing or new (to the firm) product markets (firms were about 1.5 times as likely to expand existing activities as they were to start new ones). Only 286 firms chose to withdraw products or services from some or all existing product markets, and this included 51 per cent of firms 'extremely severely' affected by the recession.[17] In fact, only 31 firms withdrew product lines without, at the same time, adding new ones (45 per cent of these firms were 'extremely severely' affected), suggesting that much of the trauma of closure and the cutbacks in plant/machinery investments did not carry forward into a wholesale narrowing of firm's product lines. Since 222 firms added to their product range without withdrawing existing products or services while 266 both introduced some new products and withdrew some existing ones, it is difficult to conclude that, on balance, product variety did not increase in many markets during the recession. Since

Table 4.9 Product market strategy

'In the period 1990–92 did your company'	% all firms		% 'extremely severely' affected firms	
	Yes	No	Yes	No
Introduce new product lines or services within existing product markets?	75	21	67	32
Introduce new product lines or services into product markets new to your company?	48	49	37	62
Leave the range of products or services supplied unchanged?	15	81	19	79
Withdraw product lines or services but continued in all product markets?	26	57	24	62
Withdraw from supplying product lines or services from some product markets?	31	54	36	51

rationalising product lines is (or should) be a key part of a *focus* strategy, these observations reinforce one's sense that many managers equate *focus* strategies with headcount reductions and plant closures.

In sum, while recessionary pressures usually have an adverse effect on investment in plant and equipment, focusing only on this type of investment activity gives a rather distorted view of the kinds of investment activities which firms undertake during recessions. Our data on the investment plans of firms during the recession leads to the conclusion that firms are much less likely to abandon or postpone investments in intangibles than they are to abandon or postpone investment in plant and machinery. More firms brought forward new product and process innovations than abandoned them and, at least partly as a consequence, more firms broadened their product lines than restricted them. Needless to say, firms who were *'extremely severely'* affected by the recession were less likely to bring forward investment than other firms but, even so, more of them brought forward investments in new product innovation than abandoned them.

Inter-firm differences in responses to the recession

The observation that the formulation and implementation of corporate strategy is a process which couples external opportunities with internal resources and capabilities is a commonplace one. It does, however, carry the strong implication that the responses which different firms make to the same set of adverse circumstances are likely to differ from each other. For example, firms with marketing skills that have been used to create product differentiation advantages are likely to respond differently to a decline in demand from firms who have invested heavily in process engineering to create a position of cost leadership. Similarly, firms with very decentralised corporate structures and parenting relationships between corporate headquarters and business units that rely almost entirely on accounting based systems of performance assessment are likely to behave quite differently from functionally organised firms whose top management is intimately familiar with the small collection of businesses they control. Indeed, the skills base of many firms operating in the same industry is often fairly idiosyncratic, and it is by no means clear that the expectation of a common, industry-wide response to recessionary pressures is a reasonable one.

However interesting these observations seem to be, a little reflection suggests that they are not particularly useful. It is relatively easy to spot differences in the internal resources and capabilities of different firms, and the prediction that each firm will respond in its own idiosyncratic fashion to adversity provides almost no guide for further study. What is more, there is apparently no end to the list of differences between firms which one might cite to explain observed differences in response to the recession. Thus, in what follows, we propose to focus on a restricted version of this argument, namely that large firms respond differently from small firms. What underlies this hypothesis is the conjecture that as firms get larger, they become progressively more difficult to manage. Although this is partly a question of sheer scale, it is also a question of diversity. Large firms are often multi-product, multi-market operators with operations spread over a wide range of activities, they frequently have divisionalised organisational structures, and their share ownership is often highly dispersed. Our view is that although sise and diversity help to cushion large firms from some external shocks (as we saw in Chapter 3 above), those shocks which do register can have a large impact on what is often a relatively loosely controlled and somewhat heterogeneous collection of businesses. By contrast, smaller, specialised firms are often already very highly focused, and they can be very tightly controlled by a small group of shareholders working with top managers in a functionally organised structure. Although the data suggests that they are more vulnerable to recessionary pressures than larger firms, we expect them to be able to adapt more readily to external shocks, and feel less need to drastically scale back their activities. Thus, we expect to see large firms responding less to recessionary pressures than smaller firms, but we expect to observe them responding more when they are affected,

Table 4.10 A typology of responses to the recession

'Focus on core':	focus on core business *'very important'* (318 firms)
'Closed establishments':	close one or more establishments (299 firms)
'Sell-off or MBO':	sell part of operations or MBO (233 firms)
'Change structure/take-over':	change organisational structure because of merger or firm expansion (212 firms)
'Reduce union presence':	cease to recognise TU and/or repudiate union-management agreement (42 firms)
'Wage freeze':	introduce wage freeze of any length (285 firms)
'Innovators':	brought forward investment in R&D, or new prod innovation, or new process innovation (244 firms)

Note: From a sample of 586 firms.

particularly by reducing slack and refocussing their activities. Further, amongst large firms, we expect holding companies and firms with *'highly dispersed'* ownership structures to respond to recessionary pressures more often and more drastically than others.

To pursue these ideas, we constructed a set of categorical variables that identified which firms pursued a number of the strategies discussed above. Table 4.10 shows the eight responses that we focused on. These categories are not mutually exclusive, and some of them were pursued simultaneously by the same firm. In particular, *'close establishments'* was often associated with merger or acquisition induced reorganisation, as was *'sell-off or MBO'*. Surprisingly, *'wage freezes'* and *'reduce union presence'* were not often pursued jointly, and *'focus on core'* activities did not make firms more *'innovative'*.

Table 4.11 shows the relationship between the ownership structure of a firm and how it responded to the recession. The rows of the table list ownership structures which vary from tightly held ownership structures (that is UK subsidiaries of foreign firms, firms with a majority stake held by directors, and so on) to *'highly dispersed'*. It is clear at a glance that tightly held firms were less likely to cite *'focus on core business'* as an important strategic response to the recession, and they were less likely to close or sell off establishments. UK subsidiaries of foreign firms were also less likely to institute a wage freeze, while firms whose directors held a majority stake were less likely to initiate a change in structure because of merger. The likelihood of a firm bringing forward some type of innovative activity seems

Table 4.11 Responses to the recession by ownership structure

Ownership structure	I all firms	II focus on core	III closed establishments	IV sold off or MBO	V change structure/ takeover	VI reduce union presence	VII wage freeze	VIII innovators
UK subsidiary of foreign firm	17.8	18.7	14.7**	12.8**	17.7	17.4	12.8**	18.9
UK owned:								
Majority stake by directors	21.2	18.1**	18.2**	13.2**	14.6**	13.0	23.9	20.0
Minority stake by directors	14.1	15.1	14.0	12.8	18.5	15.2	16.5*	12.2
Major stake by individual person or institution	7.3	6.6	6.5	7.9	5.4	4.4	8.1	5.6
Highly dispersed	36.9	38.3	43.7**	50.4**	42.3	45.7	37.4	38.9

Notes: A t-test of differences in means between this structure and other is significant at 10 per cent; ** significant at 5 per cent.

to have been completely unrelated to ownership structure, as was the willingness to recognise (or derecognise) unions.

There is also a clear pattern of association between ownership structure and the incidence of the structural changes shown on Table 4.5. The 228 firms in our sample with 'highly dispersed' ownership patterns initiated 363 changes (1.16 per firm on average), while UK subsidiaries initiated an average of 1.07 changes per firm, director controlled firms (majority and 'significant' minority stakes) initiated 0.98 changes per firm and those with other 'significant' minority stakes initiated 1.27 changes per firm. What is more, although the incidence of sell-offs, MBOs, contracting out and closures increased with increases in the dispersion of ownership (ranking UK subsidiaries to firms that were 'highly dispersed' in order of increasing dispersion of ownership), UK subsidiaries initiated an unusually large number of sell-offs (27 per cent did so) and were more active in contracting out (37 per cent did so). Only 41 per cent of UK subsidiaries closed one or more plants (28 per cent sold off at least one plant), while 59 per cent of 'highly dispersed' firms closed a plant (54 per cent sold off one or more plants).

Firms that close or sell off establishments are also much more likely to have a divisionalised or holding company structure than to be functionally organised, as Table 4.12 shows. A much lower percentage of the

Table 4.12 Responses to the recession by organisational structure

Ownership structure	I all firms	II focus on core	III closed establishments	IV sold off or MBO	V change structure/ takeover	VI reduce union presence	VII wage freeze	VIII innova- tors
Functionally organised	33.3	29.8**	24.4**	19.4**	23.1**	13.0**	31.0	24.4**
Holding companies	34.1	33.4	39.1**	40.5**	40.0**	23.9	36.0	38.9
Divisional	27.8	30.7*	32.3**	36.0**	31.6	54.4**	30.0	32.8*

Notes: A t-test of differences in means between this structure and other is significant at 10 per cent; ** significant at 5 per cent.

population of functionally organised firms thought that *'focus on core business'* was an important response to the recession, and functionally organised firms were much less likely to reduce union presence or change their structure because of takeover than divisionalised firms or holding companies. In fact, very few functionally organised firms cited any of the *'financial responses'* listed on Table 4.1 as being very important, and they were much less likely to resort to any form of cost control than divisionalised firms and holding companies. Only 48 per cent of functionally organised firms cited *'focus on core business'* as being important, while 53 per cent of holding companies and 59 per cent of divisionalised firms did so. Further, functionally organised firms showed somewhat greater stability than holding companies and, less clearly, divisionalised firms. Of the 162 firms who did not change their organisational structure (see Table 4.6), 57 were holding companies and 22 were divisionalised firms; that is 83 functionally organised firms did not change their organisational structure (52 per cent of the population of functionally organised firms.) Finally, of the 439 slimming operations reported in Table 4.5, 265 were initiated by divisionalised firms (117 of whom sold or closed an establishment), while only 182 were initiated by functionally organised firms (only 90 of whom sold or closed an establishment). 70 per cent of the population of holding companies sold or closed an establishment. All of this is consistent with the view that functionally organised firms are much more focused than divisionalised firms or holding companies and, therefore, much less likely to undertake the kinds of slimming activities which frequently seem to be the palpable consequence of implementing focus strategies.

Table 4.13 Responses to the recession by firm size

Firm size sales	I all firms	II focus on core	III closed establishments	IV sold off or MBO	V change structure/ takeover	VI reduce union presence	VII wage freeze	VIII innovators
Sales ≤ £5 m	5.3	3.9*	2.3**	2.5**	3.9	-	5.1	4.4
£5m–£10m	6.6	5.4	5.2	6.2	11.5**	2.2**	6.4	4.4
£10m–£50m	27.7	25.3	25.4	20.7**	34.6*	13.0**	29.0	29.4
£50m–£100m	19.7	20.2	19.9	20.3*	14.6	10.9**	21.6	17.2
£100m–£500m	24.3	28.6**	27.7*	29.8**	20.8	37.0**	23.9	29.4*
£500⁺m	12.3	13.6	17.6**	18.6**	10.8	32.6**	11.1	11.1

Notes: A t-test of differences in means between this structure and other is significant at 10 per cent; ** significant at 5 per cent.

Ownership and internal organisational structures are correlated with firm size, but the fit is far from perfect (not least because the diversity of a firms operations is an important determinant of organisational structure). Nevertheless, as Table 4.13 shows, the patterns of response linked with ownership and internal organisational structure are roughly similar to those linked with firm size. Smaller firms were much less likely to think that 'focus on core business' was an important response to the recession than larger firms, and they were less likely to close or sell off plants. They were also much less likely to reduce union presence than larger firms, slightly more likely to change their structure due to a merger and somewhat less likely to be innovative. There is no obvious relationship in the data between firm size and the imposition of a wage freeze, but firm size is an important determinant of the likelihood that a firm has changed its organisational structure. For example, the 76 firms in our data with sales in excess of £500m initiated 159 of the structural changes recorded on Table 4.6 (an average of 2 per firm over an eight year period). By contrast, the 74 firms with sales less than £10m initiated only 59 structural changes in total (an average of 0.8 per firm). Very large firms with sales in excess of £500m displayed a marked propensity to contract out services (58 per cent did so) and to close establishments (71 per cent did so). Smaller firms with sales less than £10m were much less likely to close plants (only 31 per cent did so).

It also turns out to be the case that there are other characteristics of firms that seem to be associated with the use of particular strategies. Firms with relatively new CEOs (that is with tenure of five years or less) were much more likely to close or sell off establishments and focus on core businesses than those with long serving CEOs (that is with tenure of 11 years or more). Firms that grew rapidly before the recession and had relatively low profit margins were also likely to focus on core business, close or sell off establishments and freeze wages, as were firms with high debt/assets ratios and low cash/liabilities ratios. Surprisingly, firms with employee share ownership schemes were rather more likely to close or sell off establishments, and they tended to derecognise unions more frequently than the average.

The evidence, then, suggests that there is a considerable heterogeneity in the response of firms to recessionary pressures, and that at least some of these differences are associated with the size of firms and with their ownership and internal organisational structures. Large firms with highly dispersed ownership structures and organised as holding companies or divisionalised firms were much more likely to change the structure of their companies or to close or sell off businesses than smaller functionally organised firms with tighter ownership structures were. This is, in part, a consequence of the fact that holding companies and firms with 'highly dispersed' ownership structures (but not firms with high turnover) were somewhat more vulnerable to the recession. However, these observations do not explain everything that we observe. The data are also consistent with the view that many firms grew overlarge in the 1980s, becoming too big and too diversified to manage properly and outgrowing their ownership base in a way which made the efficient monitoring of managers by shareholders more difficult.[18] For at least some of these firms, the recession in the early 1990s provided an opportunity to make some much needed adjustments to what seems to have been an unbalanced and unsustainable corporate growth programme.

Conclusions

The data which we have discussed in this chapter show fairly clearly that the main response to recessionary pressures initiated by the firms in our sample was to attack costs, and this means that the typical structural change initiated in a recession was driven by a desire to reduce headcount (protestations about increasing *focus* notwithstanding). Many firms shut establishments and most shed labour, some trimmed headquarters costs, reduced inventories and postponed or abandoned investments. More interestingly (and less obviously driven by headcount), a substantial number of firms brought forward a range of investments in human, technological and marketing capital during recessions. Although investments in all forms of capital typically fell, a surprisingly large number of firms brought forward investments in intangibles like R&D, training and marketing, and even more brought forward product and process innovations. Finally, recessions are a time when many firms reorganise their activities and their organisational structures (often in response to over expansion), but the data suggest that it is not the only time when this happens (nor the most important).

The frequency with which firms resort to cost cutting measures in the recession is a little puzzling, since one expects that profit maximising firms will attempt to reduce costs at all times. Nor is it immediately obvious why a firm's first and most important response to decline in demand is to cut cost. Further, many firms who cut costs by shedding labour or closing establishments did not also narrow their product lines or withdraw from less profitable markets. It is, of course, possible that shedding labour or closing establishments are relatively inexpensive responses to hard times, but the fact that they can often have an immediate and beneficial effect on cash flow raises the question of whether they are simply the consequence of myopic decision making.

It is also worth re-emphasising the heterogeneity of responses that we have observed in the data. It turns out that trying to identify which firms were forced to take drastic actions and which firms did not is rather difficult. There are, however, some systematic patterns in the data. One can organise the various responses that we have observed in various ways, but the use of firm size yields particularly interesting results. Although it is not obviously the case that large firms were more adversely affected by the recession than small firms, the fact is that large firms responded more actively than small firms. 'Large' in the sense that we have used it here also refers to 'highly dispersed' ownership structures and the use of holding company or divisionalised structures to enable top managers to control the constituent parts of their empires. It is not hard to believe that these large firms are less focused and less tightly managed/controlled than smaller, functionalised firms with less dispersed ownership structures. Given this very casual empirical judgement, it would seem that the relatively high incidence of change reported by large firms is consistent with the view that recessions cut into fat. Put another way, it seems that at times of maximum selection pressure, large firms (and particularly holding companies with highly dispersed share ownership) do not reveal themselves to be particularly fit or competitive.

One final comment is in order. The primary responses to the recession that we have observed are mostly about controlling costs: closure of establishments, shedding labour, wage freezes and postponed investments in capital. What is more, these cost control responses are all strongly related to the severity of the impact of the recession on the firm. However, we have observed other responses, such as bringing forward new products or processes, expanding the range of products, changing organisational structures, reducing union presence and so on, which are not obviously related to the severity of impact of the recession on the individual firm who took one or more of these actions. Further, as we shall see below, predicting the incidence of some of these other changes is very difficult. This observation raises the moot point of whether some or all of these probably productivity enhancing changes are truly a consequence of the recession. Certainly, many of the organisational changes we observed were not induced by the recession (mergers, in particular, are a major cause of company reorganisation). Recessions seem to be important only as a driver of changes in labour organisation and plant closure and do not appear to initiate more fundamental changes on the supply side of the economy. Some cleansing occurs during downturns in economic activity, but it can hardly be described as a fully loaded machine wash.

5 The labour market in recession

Introduction

Almost all markets are connected to other markets. Substitution by consumers links horizontally related markets (similar products in the same location, same product in different locations), while strategic actions by firms operating in one particular product market affect vertically related markets up and down the value chain. To understand the full effects that recessions have, one needs to trace demand shocks in particular product markets upward and outward throughout the economy. Many of the most visible of these knock-on effects appear in the labour market, and that is the subject of this chapter.

As we have seen (in Chapter 4), the evidence suggests that the most common response which firms make to recessionary pressures is to cut costs. Further, most cost cutting measures seem to centre on job shedding, curbing wages growth and plant closure, actions that are often described as '*increasing focus*' but which sometimes look like being head count driven or motivated by a concern with short-term cash flow. In principle, costs can be reduced by cutting wage costs per head or reducing labour input and, in fact, there is a large literature which suggests that firms might prefer to adjust quantities rather than prices, a proposition consistent with the rather weak cyclical variation in real wages which we observe over the trade cycle.[1] It is, however, worth using our microeconomic data to ask whether wage freezes and lay-offs are actually complements, since firms that desperately need to reduce their costs will presumably try to do so in any way that they can. Further, there are numerous ways to cut wages (reduce overtime, reduce piece rates, institute a wage freeze, sack older workers or shift from full-time to part-time employment) and to reduce labour input (close whole plants, cull less efficient workers, reduce shifts or implement involuntary holidays), and it is not at all clear which choices firms should and actually do make.

One question of considerable interest in this respect is whether the responses to shocks made by firms (be they of prices or of quantities) are frequent but gradual (smoothing out changes over time), or infrequent but large (cumulating differences between desired and actual levels of employment, wages growth or whatever, until a certain threshold is past which induces a single, large response). This turns on the nature of adjustment costs, and whether they are fixed or vary with the size of the adjustments made. Econometric practice tends to presume that adjustment costs are variable and, therefore, that the adjustment to shocks is gradual, but this is at least partly a matter of analytical convenience. The hypothesis of gradual adjustment often seems to be a reasonable representation of aggregate data, but there is a growing suspicion this may be an artifact of aggregation and not a good description of what individual firms actually do. One of our goals in what follows, then, is to examine not only the incidence of price and quantity changes, but also the specific methods used to implement them and their relative frequency of use at a very microeconomic level.

Changes in wages and employment are part of a much wider, and possibly more profound set of structural changes in the labour market which can be induced by recessionary pressures. Whenever markets are in disarray, agents will have strong incentives to mould market institutions (or create new ones) to minimise transactions costs. Further, major changes in cost or demand conditions affect the relative bargaining power of workers and managers. Falling orders and rising levels of inventories reduce the costs to employers of strikes or other disputes which disrupt current production. Indeed, the threat of bankruptcy may lead to wholesale changes in wage rates, wage structures and working practices in an effort to save jobs. Further, growing unemployment and the slowdown in wage growth elsewhere in the economy reduce the force of threats to quit and the pressures created by changes in relative wages. All of these changes will also affect decisions by firms to recognise unions, and decisions by workers to join them. These changes are, in turn, likely to induce changes in bargaining structures.[2] One of our goals in what follows is to document recent changes in union recognition, union density and wage bargaining structures, and to assess the degree to which the Major-Lamont recession hastened or retarded trends evident for the last decade or so.

The plan is as follows. We start by examining the incidence of job shedding and the control of wages growth using data from our survey. We then supplement this with information obtained from an earlier survey undertaken by one of the authors in 1990. Taken together, the two surveys will enable us to examine trends in union recognition, union membership and wage setting arrangements from the mid to late 1980s, and make a fairly precise assessment of the impact that the recession had on these structures.[3]

Employment and wages

Most people believe that job losses are a phenomena of recessions, and that booms are periods in which job are created. However, this is only true in aggregate. As we saw earlier (see Table 4.3 in particular), job losses were most in evidence in 1981, and 1991–2; by contrast, employment grew on average by 9 per cent in 1988 prior to the recession, and by not much less in 1987 and 1989. A closer look at the data, however, reveals that these averages give a misleading impression of what happens to many firms over the cycle. Even in the most prosperous boom years, around 30 per cent of firms shed labour. On the other hand, in the depths of a recession year like 1981, 25 per cent of firms did not shed labour, and in 1991 and 1992 only 60 per cent of firms reduced employment. Thus, the swing from boom to bust moved about 20 per cent of firms from expansion to contraction of employment, but still left plenty of firms doing one thing or the other (or both in different establishments, or with respect to different types of jobs). What is more, employment growth and contraction are highly concentrated on a small number of firms who experienced big changes in employment in booms and recessions. The difference between the recession years 1989–92 and the boom years 1986–9 was that about 30 more firms shed more than 1,000 employees, and 30 less firms expanded by more than a 1,000 employees. About 75 per cent of the jobs shed by firms in any year came from firms who initiated contractions of 1,000 employees or more. In the boom year of 1988, around one in eight firms shed 10 per cent or more of its labour force, while in a recession year of 1991 one in four firms shed 10 per cent or more of their employees (in 1981, one in three shed 10 per cent or more). The variation in the proportion of firms shedding 1,000 or more of their employees over time is much more muted than this, moving from about one in eight to one in six across the cycle.[4]

The data generated by our survey also has these features. As we noted in Chapter 3, just under half of the 586 core firms responding to our survey reduced employment in response to the recession, and they considered it to be a *very important* part of their overall response to the pressures they faced. Further, 17 out of 19 firms reporting extreme distress but not saying that employment reduction was *very important* said that they

Table 5.1 Pay growth and the use of wage freezes

| | Wage bill growth per employee | | | | | |
| | All firms | | Union | | Non-union | |
	Median wage growth 1990–92	No. of firms	Median wage growth 1990–92	No. of firms	Median wage growth 1990–92	No. of firms
Did you operate a wage freeze?						
No	16.3%	263	16.2%	144	16.3%	119
Yes	14.3%	275	15.2%	125	13.6%	150
Of what length?						
3 months or less	16.1%	16	16.9%	8	15.1%	8
4-6 months	14.3%	55	15.8%	41	11.5%	14
7-11 months	16.1%	95	15.3%	42	17.9%	53
12+ months	11.7%	109	11.4%	34	12.0%	75
All firms	15.6%	547	15.9%	273	14.6%	281

reduced employment and that it was at least of 'some importance'. The median firm among those who were 'extremely severely' affected by the recession contracted by 22 per cent, the median 'severely' affected firm contracted by 7 per cent, while those that were 'moderately' or 'not at all' affected actually grew marginally. The median firm reporting job shedding as an important response typically reduced employment between 1989 and 1992 by 13 per cent, while in those not citing job shedding as an important response employment typically grew by 3 per cent. The quintile of firms who shed most jobs accounted for 94 per cent of all job losses reported by our firms.

There are many ways for firms to control wages growth, but the 1990 recession saw something of an innovation in this respect. Concession bargaining was rare in the UK during the early 1980s, but 48 per cent of the firms in our sample operated a temporary wage freeze in the period 1990–93. Further, 54 per cent of non-union firms did so, while only 44 per cent of union firms did, and the wage freezes operated by non-union firms were longer on average. Wage freezes seem to have been the major method of wage growth control used by the firms in our sample, and Table 5.1 shows wage growth across firms according to whether they operated a wage freeze or not, and by the length of the freeze if one was operated. Over 37 per cent of firms operated a freeze which lasted more than 6 months, while only 3 per cent operated one lasting less than 3 months. Further, and rather more interestingly, job shedding and wage growth reduction occurred mainly in

Table 5.2 *Which firms shed the jobs regressions of change in ln (employment) 1992, 1989*

	(1)	(2)
'Extremely severely' affected	−0.2609	−0.2479
	(0.0654)	(0.0639)
'Severely' affected	−0.1366	−0.1147
	(0.0506)	(0.0473)
Closure of establishments	−0.0812	−0.0772
(Very important response)	(0.0477)	(0.0459)
Wage growth reductions	−0.0039	0.0121
(Very important response)	(0.0456)	(0.0466)
Recognised trade union	0.1084	0.0780
	(0.0442)	(0.0458)
Ln(average employment 1985–9)	−0.0352	0.0385
	(0.0158)	(0.0156)
Ln(emp 1989)–ln(emp 1986)	0.0158	0.0240
	(0.0358)	(0.0364)
Cash/liabilities 1989	0.0971	0.1280
	(0.0787)	(0.0780)
Average profit margin 1985–9	0.1944	0.4710
	(0.1754)	(0.2017)
Constant	0.2138	0.3393
	(0.1230)	(0.2000)
Industry dummies included	No	Yes
Number obs.	514	514
R^2	0.090	0.149

Note: Heteroscedastic consistent standard errors in brackets.

the same firms: among the 286 firms reporting job shedding as important, 192 also reported wage growth reduction as important (only 94 did not) Likewise, of the 227 firms for whom wage growth reductions were an important response, only 35 did not cite employment reductions as also being important. Among firms citing job shedding as important, median employment shedding was 14 per cent in those firms who also reported wage growth reduction, but only 11 per cent among those who did not. That is, firms who emphasised wage growth reductions as being very important typically shed more labour than those who did not. There are at least three reasons why this is the case.

The most obvious explanation of the positive correlation between the incidence of job shedding and wage growth reduction that we see in the data is that it reflects the severity of the impact of the recession. That is, those firms using wage growth reductions and employment reductions are likely to have been the most hard hit by the recession. Table 5.2 reports two OLS regressions explaining the change in the log of employment between 1989 and 1992 reported by firms. The two specifications differ only by the inclusion of industry dummies in the second specification. Both regressions show that after controlling for the severity of the impact of the recession, firms citing reduced wage growth as an important response to the recession had no significant differences in the extent of job losses. Much the same applied in other regressions which included variables recording the use of a wage freeze and measuring its duration. Unsurprisingly, plant closure was correlated with greater job shedding, and larger firms shed more jobs than smaller ones. Firms that were profitable prior to the recession and those that were cash rich were less likely to shed labour than others. These results are consistent with the argument that firms were willing to use internal funds to smooth adjustments in the employment levels but found it difficult to use externally supplied funds for this purpose. Unionised firms also shed fewer jobs, although this effect was borderline in terms of statistical significance when industry dummies are included.

Second, wage growth reduction does not seem to mitigate the extent of job loss much because the variation in wage growth between firms citing reductions in wage growth and those that did not was small. As we saw in Table 5.1, firms operating a freeze experienced wages growth between 1990 and 1992 which was just 2 per cent lower than in other firms. Only among firms operating a freeze for more than a year (that is, in about one in five firms) was wage growth substantially lower than this. Given standard estimates of the sensitivity of employment to real wages of 0.5 or less, then the 2 percentage point difference in wage growth should generate only a 1 per cent difference in employment growth. The variation in employment growth between those cutting costs through job shedding and those who did not was, however, 16 percentage points. Hence, wage freezes were very much a second order of importance in cost control relative to employment shedding.

Third, and probably of lesser importance, the fact that reductions in wage growth and in employment seem to be used together may reflect the role played by unions in the adjustment process. It is widely believed that unions increase costs of adjustment (through manning agreements or higher redundancy costs), and they may also increase the cost of actions such as real wage cuts (by inducing strikes or other forms of shopfloor disruption).[5] Unionised firms achieved on average a 1.5 per cent larger increase in wages relative to non-union firms over the period covered by our survey (see Table 5.1). This difference seems to be mainly due to the difference between

union and non-union firms in the use of wage freezes, and their shorter duration (note particularly the lower propensity for unionised firms to
experience wage freezes of 12 months plus). This is consistent with evidence
that the union wage mark-up is countercyclical.[6] Further, in the downturn,
unionised firms did not reduce employment as much as non-union firms.
This may help to induce the positive correlation between job shedding and
control of wages growth that we have observed. What is more, these two
effects imply that unionised firms will have lower profitability (and perhaps productivity) relative to non-union firms in the recession years. This
said, the effects of unionisation on both wages and employment adjustment
were small and, therefore, the importance of unions in labour market adjustment in the recession was very much a second order effect. For this
reason, the impact of unions on firm failure is likely to be small. Receivership was rare among firms not making losses, and even then it was confined
to smaller firms and those with heavy debt loads. Union presence is generally highest in larger, older and slower growing firms.

These results are interesting not so much because they are consistent with
the hypothesis that firms are quantity adjusters, as because they are inconsistent with the view that firms adjust quantities but not prices. In fact, our
data suggest that while quantity adjustments were dominant, the use of
wage freezes and lay-offs or plant closures were complementary methods
of controlling costs. 'Extremely severely' affected firms used virtually any
instrument that they could to reduce costs (particularly if they did not face
a strong union), and this was also true for many of the less severely affected
firms who tried to control costs. The relative importance of quantity responses at least partly reflects the fact that, in a period of low inflation,
reducing wage growth by wage freezes is unlikely to have much effect on
real wages. It also arises because the apparently preferred method of shedding labour (namely plant closure) has a very much larger effect on costs
than wage freezes. As a way of getting the job done, it is quick and effective, and it reduces the need to use other instruments.

Employment shedding is largely driven by a small number of firms who
need to make a radical alteration in their costs. The 560 firms who answered
our survey and have complete employment data for 1989 through to 1992
collectively shed just over 200,000 jobs. However, only around 60 per cent
of these firms actually shed labour, and the total jobs lost among these firms
was 383,000. Nearly 90 per cent of the lost jobs occurred in just 56 firms
(that is, in 10 per cent of the sample). Every firm in this bottom decile shrunk
by 40 per cent or more. That is, job losses in recessions (and, less clearly,
job gains in booms) are not the sum of many marginal adjustments towards
changed target levels of employment.[7] In fact, job loss is bound up with

plant closure, which is also highly concentrated in a minority of firms. Amongst other things, this suggests that the typical response of firms to shocks is large, infrequent and discrete, not frequent and gradual; that is, individual firms do not appear to smooth their responses to shocks over time This, in turn, implies that adjustment costs are likely to be relatively independent of the size of the adjustment made by a firm. Further, the fact that smooth or gradual adjustment to shocks is an apparently accurate description of movements in aggregate employment raises concerns about aggregation bias: what looks at a macroeconomic level as the gradual adjustment of employment to changes in demand by all firms is, in fact, the result of very large employment changes initiated by a few firms.[8]

Union recognition

There is a widely held belief that the influence of trade unionism has been on the wane in the UK since 1979. The most notable manifestation of this decline is a continued erosion in trade union membership, which dropped from a high of around 13.3 million in 1979 to 9.0 million by 1993. Further, new recognitions of unions by firms became increasingly less frequent and derecognitions somewhat less rare in the later part of the 1980s. All of this is consistent with a perceptible shift in relative bargaining power between management and unions in the 1980s, aided and abetted by a rash of legislation introduced by the Thatcher government. The UK recession of the early 1980s and the high unemployment levels which persisted through the 1980s almost certainly continued the erosion in the relative bargaining power of unions and it is, therefore, worth asking whether managers took the opportunity to consolidate their position by derecognising unions.

To examine the question of whether (and to what extent) these changes were accelerated by the recession, it is useful to push beyond the single cross section of our survey. We have, therefore, extended our data to include the results of a survey undertaken by Gregg and Yates, 1991, designed to explore issues about union presence and pay-setting systems in firms. This first survey was undertaken in the spring of 1990, and contacted firms who were trading in 1988. The sampling frames of the two surveys differ only because of entry and exit between 1988 and 1990. We made an attempt to produce a panel by making extra efforts to secure responses (in 1993) on at least the industrial relations questions from respondents to the 1990 survey. Of the 515 firms who responded to the first survey and were still trading in 1993, 235 also responded to the second survey (a response rate

Table 5.3 *Union recognition 1990, 1993, by number of establishments in the company*

Establishments operated	1990		1993	
	No union recognition	Unions recognised	No union recognition	Unions recognised
1	61% (61)	37% (37)	70% (54)	30% (23)
More than 1 of which:	44% (200)	56 (256)	48% (257)	52% (271)
2-5	51% (92)	49% (87)	58% (117)	42% (86)
6-10	43% (39)	57% (52)	47% (51)	53% (57)
11-20	37% (24)	63% (41)	46% (33)	54% (39)
21+	35% (38)	65% (72)	35% (42)	65% (78)
Unknown	64% (7)	36% (4)	56% (14)	44% (11)
All companies	47.1% (261)	52.9% (293)	51.4% (311)	48.6% (294)

of 45.6 per cent). To examine the effect of the recession on union recognition, we asked firms who participated in both surveys whether they: *recognised trade unions for the purposes of bargaining over wages in any of your establishments* (firms who adhered to national agreements without recognising or bargaining with union representatives were advised to respond negatively). 48.6 per cent of the 605 firms responding to the 1993 survey indicated that they did recognise at least one union in 1993. The corresponding figure for the 1990 survey was 52.9 per cent. Table 5.3 gives a breakdown of union recognition across the number of plants operated by each firm who responded to both of the 1990 and 1993 surveys. A pattern of declining recognition over time appears to be common across all groups of firms, except those with the largest number of plants. The existence of a higher propensity to recognise unions in firms with more establishments is, however, common to both samples.

There are three possible causes of the changes recorded in the table: they may arise from the change in the sampling frame between the two surveys (that is, sample attrition), they may be driven by differential response rates for firms with characteristics associated with recognition (for example, more small firms responded to the second survey for a common sampling frame) and finally some firms may have derecognised unions between 1990 and 1993. Let us consider each cause in turn.

Table 5.4 gives details of union recognition for entrants into EXSTAT between 1988 and 1990 (the dates of the two EXSTAT sampling frames used in the 1990 and 1993 surveys respectively), and exits from the sample since 1988. Only 13 of the 29 entrant firms who responded to the survey

Table 5.4 *Changes in the sampling frame between 1988 and 1990*

	No union recognition		Union recognition	
	N	%	N	%
Firms who entered				
EXSTAT after 1988	16	55	13	45
Firms who exited the				
EXSTAT sample by 1993	54	48	58	52
Firms who exited EXSTAT				
through deselection 1988–90	6	29	15	71
Firms who exited EXSTAT				
through TAKEOVER 1988–93	39	55	32	45
Firms who exited EXSTAT				
through RECEIVERSHIP				
1990–93	9	45	11	55
Survivors New	285	50.8	276	49.2
Old	209	47.0	235	53.0

Note: Deselection occurs when EXSTAT removes a company from the database. This typically occurs when a subsidiary (often of a foreign multinational) ceases to report separate accounts. Some of the companies taken over will have been bought out of receivership. N = number of companies.

in 1993 (there were 132 entrants in total) recognised a union (45 per cent).[9] This is a little lower than the average figure for all firms in 1993. Keeping track of exiting firms is a little more difficult. One hundred and nine companies who responded to our first survey ceased to trade or were taken over at some time after 1988, but 15 of them still managed to respond to our enquiries in 1993. Further, three of the responding firms to our 1993 survey ceased independent trading after 1990. Union recognition was 52 per cent across all exitor firms, but there were differences between those firms who had been taken over and those who went into receivership (45 per cent and 55 per cent respectively recognised unions). However, delisted firms (a diverse category containing mostly subsidiaries of foreign companies that ceased reporting separate accounts) had the highest union recognition rates of all (71 per cent). It follows, then, that exitors were a little more likely to recognise unions than entrants were but, nevertheless, the changing sample composition explains relatively little of the total shift away from unionisation observed by comparing the two surveys. Concentrating only on survivors, the gap in the proportion of firms which recognised unions between the 1990 and the 1993 samples is still 3.8 percentage points, as compared with 4.3 percentage points for all firms.

A second explanation of the observed decline in union recognition between the two surveys is that different types of company responded to the
two surveys, implying that the observed decline in union recognition may
be an artifact of sampling rather than a genuine change in the extent of
recognition. We address this issue by decomposing the overall change in
union recognition into that explained by different characteristics of firms,
and that explained by different propensities to recognise a union given a
firm's characteristics.[10] The first step in this process is to examine the determinants of the probability that a firm recognised unions. Then, using
these regressions, one can compute how much more or less likely firms with
different characteristics (that is, different values of the independent variables) were to recognise unions. Separate probit equations explaining the
probability that a firm recognised a union were estimated for surviving firms
from the two surveys (that is, for those firms trading independently throughout the 1988–93 period). These are shown on Table 5.5. The estimated
equations control for date of incorporation of the firm, sales, number of
plants and the diversity of product markets in which the firm operates; industry controls are also included. Broadly speaking, the results contain no
surprises. Union recognition was more common amongst larger firms, and
occurs principally in firms with sales of over £100 million in 1989. Union
recognition was less likely in firms whose date of incorporation was more
recent, especially those incorporated in the 1970s and 1980s (but with
little difference between these two periods).

The second step is to compare the characteristics of firms in the two samples and, having isolated the differences between them, compute how big
an effect these differences had on the probability of recognising a union.
The results of the decomposition suggest that around 60 per cent of the decline in union recognition amongst the surviving firms of the two surveys
arises from different firm characteristics. Further, it turns out that firm size
alone explains almost all of this difference: that is, the 1993 sample had
more small firms responding than in the 1990 survey, and small firms were
less likely to recognise unions. The rest of the observed decline in union
recognition is attributable to a decline in the propensity to recognise
unions by firms with given characteristics. The biggest shifts toward lower
recognition in 1993 were recorded by small firms (annual sales <50m),
single plant firms, firms in 'other services' and firms with dates of incorporation prior to World War I.

The third possible cause of the changes in union recognition shown on
Table 5.3 is that firms may have chosen to withdraw union recognition in
their plants. Both of our surveys asked whether: *any union in any plant
had been derecognised for the purposes of bargaining over wages* (changes

Table 5.5 Probit estimates of union recognition

Variable	1990	1990	1993	1993
2–5 plants	−0.0163	−0.1486	0.1493	0.0429
	(0.2135)	(0.2314)	(0.2025)	(0.2145)
6+ plants	0.0276	−0.0081	0.2589	0.4437
	(0.2092)	(0.2287)	(0.1998)	(0.2145)
Plant no. N/A	−0.1957	−0.3317	−0.2049	−0.3215
	(0.5519)	(0.6261)	(0.4264)	(0.4855)
Sales £5–10m	−0.4831	−0.2782	0.0048	0.2130
	(0.5724)	(0.6179)	(0.4009)	(0.4516)
Sales £10–50m	0.4211	0.2481	0.6017	0.5891
	(0.4867)	(0.5316)	(0.3237)	(0.3654)
Sales £50–100m	0.3331	0.1906	0.8731	0.9419
	(0.5019)	(0.5492)	(0.3317)	(0.3734)
Sales £100–500m	0.6977	0.6154	1.229	1.340
	(0.4869)	(0.5335)	(0.3285)	(0.3712)
Sales £500m+	1.324	1.412	1.922	2.037
	(0.5113)	(0.5592)	(0.3702)	(0.4211)
Formed 1919–45	−1.225	−1.081	−0.2970	−0.1043
	(0.2541)	(0.2789)	(0.1962)	(0.2138)
Formed 1945–69	−1.397	−1.409	−0.4160	−0.2773
	(0.2481)	(0.2761)	(0.1929)	(0.2120)
Formed 1970–79	−1.555	−1.548	−0.7780	0.4742
	(0.2784)	(0.3063)	(0.2238)	(0.2448)
Formed 1980–89	−1.168	−1.052	−0.5871	−0.2658
	(0.2559)	(0.2908)	(0.1902)	(0.2129)
Diverse products	0.2968	0.1309	0.3486	0.1900
	(0.1441)	(0.1574)	(0.1240)	(0.1366)
Energy		0.1975		0.7160
		(0.5319)		(0.4677)
Chemicals		0.3820		1.005
		(0.4258)		(0.3514)
Engineering		−0.0064		0.6175
		(0.3801)		(0.3138)
Other manufacturing		0.8831		1.165
		(0.3893)		(0.3247)
Construction		−0.2311		0.2725
		(0.4498)		(−0.3667)
Retail		−0.6743		−0.3289
		(0.3689)		(0.3051)
Transport		−0.7068		0.1915
		(0.5003)		(0.4142)
Business services		−0.9294		−0.6068
		(0.4061)		(0.3413)
Constant	0.4799	0.8041	−0.8948	−1.410
	(0.5334)	(0.6452)	(0.3752)	(0.4928)
No. of obs.	410	410	541	541
R^2	0.178	0.298	0.173	0.294

Table 5.6 Changes in union recognition, 1985–93

	1990–93		1985–90		1990–93 panel	
	N	%	N	%	N	%
No change or presence increased	255	42	253	45	116	50
At least one TU derecognised but unions still recognised	36	6	33	6	–	–
All TU derecognised	8	1	7	1	5	2
Never recognised	282	47	185	33	108	49
Changes not reported	25	4	80	14	1	0
Changes in union status without changes in recognition:						
Increases	–	–	–	–	3	1
Decreases	–	–	–	–	4	2

Note. The vast majority of non-respondents did not recognise trade unions at the end of either period. In the panel, 4 firms removed trade unions other than by derecognition, 2 disposed of the unionised part of the company and 2 gave no information. The 4 companies that increased recognition included 2 who indicated this was due to takeover of a unionised company. There were no acknowledged increases through new recognition in the panel. N = number of companies.

in union presence due to union merger or plant closure were excluded). The 1990 survey revealed that between 1985 and 1989 a total of 40 companies (around 14 per cent of all unionised companies) engaged in at least partial derecognition. However, in only seven firms did this result in total derecognition (see the third column of Table 5.6). The 1993 survey shows that the period since 1990 saw a similar degree of derecognition (see the first column of Table 5.6). Forty-three firms derecognised at least one union (again, around 14 per cent of all unionised companies), including 8 who initiated a total derecognition (3 per cent of union firms). Although the numbers are similar in the two surveys, the second time period is much shorter and, therefore, implies a faster rate of decline. Firms who partially derecognised their unions were concentrated in the energy, construction and transport sectors, and they were likely to be both larger and older than the average unionised firm. Firms engaged in total derecognition were somewhat more likely to be in manufacturing, but they were much smaller in size than the average unionised firm: half of these firms had sales of less than £50 million, whereas only a quarter of all unionised firms were this small.[11]

The vast majority of firms who replied to both surveys had the same union status in both periods, but 12 firms indicated differences in their union recognition: 9 away from union recognition and 3 towards it. We contacted these firms by phone or letter seeking confirmation of these changes, and whether they constituted derecognition. Five of the nine firms who moved away from recognised unions between 1990 and 1993 said they had derecognised for the purposes of wage bargaining (although two of them indicated that unions were still present and were consulted on other issues), and two said they had disposed of part of the organisation that had union recognition (the other two firms did not respond). Four of the five firms derecognising unions had sales below the median for unionised companies (that is, less than £175 million), all but one was in non-manufacturing and two had previously reported partial derecognition prior to 1990. It is worth noting that estimates of the extent of complete union derecognition from both the 1993 survey and the panel were between 3 and 4 per cent of unionised firms (and were largely confined to smaller firms). Of the three firms who moved toward recognised unions over the period 1990–93, two indicated that they had done so because they acquired an organisation with union recognition, and the other one gave no response.[12]

In short, if the union recognition rate had been the same in the 1993 survey as it was in the 1990 survey, then 320 firms out of 605 responding would have recognised unions. We actually observed that only 294 firms recognised unions. Sample attrition only accounts for three of the 26 firm shortfall (12 per cent), whilst differing characteristics accounts for nine firms (35 per cent). This decline in measured recognition is almost certainly due to different response rates for small firms and, as such, probably does not represent a decline in underlying union presence. The largest factor responsible for the gap is a change in the propensity of firms to recognise unions, accounting for fourteen firms (53 per cent) or around 4 per cent of the stock of union firms.[13] All in all, it seems reasonable to conclude that few firms were either willing or able to translate shifts in bargaining power away from unionised labour into permanent reductions in the presence of unions in their establishments.

Union membership and wage setting arrangements

Whether a company recognises a union is one thing; the purposes for which the company recognises it and the shop floor level of support which union

Table 5.7 *Level of union membership density in 1990 and 1993*

	1990			1993		
	U	W	N	U	W	N
Union recognition:						
No	1.9	1.6	225	2.7	3.8	275
Yes, without closed shop	53.4	60.9	193	43.7	50.5	202
Yes, with closed shop	54.9	53.3	59	55.0	54.4	49
Total	29.3	53.1	477	23.5	46.0	529

Note: N = number of firms, U = unweighted average union density and W = weighted average union density (weights were company employment in 1990, or 1989 if 1990 data not available).

leaders enjoy are other things altogether. Since it is hard to believe that the apparently large shifts in union relative bargaining power which occurred throughout the 1980s, and which were deepened in the 1990–92 recession, did not have a major effect on industrial relations systems, the very modest decline in union recognition which we observed above suggests that some other change may have made derecognition relatively unimportant or unnecessary. One possibility is that union membership dropped, making recognised unions into little more than hollow shells; another is that wage setting (or other bargaining) arrangements changed in a way which undermined the leverage which unions have traditionally brought to the bargaining table. The most obvious example of this kind of change is a shift away from national or multi-employer wage setting towards local, plant level bargaining.

Table 5.7 displays data on union membership generated by the two surveys. The overall fall in union membership was 7 per cent when each firm is weighted by its employment in 1990.[14] The presence of a closed shop or a union-management agreement on membership seemed to make little difference to the degree of union density, probably because only a minority of workers are covered by these agreements. Surprisingly, the presence of union members in firms without union recognition appears to have risen slightly. Table 5.8 shows the decline in union density across the different possible patterns of union recognition in 1990 and 1993 from the panel. The small number of firms with increased union presence combined with their low employment levels seems to be behind what is only a tiny increase in union membership, a change that is easily offset by decreases in union

Table 5.8 Changes in the level of union density 1990, 1993

| Recognition in | | % changes in density | | Contribution to change |
1990	1993	U	W	across all firms
No	Yes, new union presence	35.0	24.0	+0.04
Yes	Yes, no change in union presence	−3.7	−6.7	−5.29
Yes	Yes, partial derecognition	−17.5	−16.7	−1.82
Yes	No, total derecognition	−16.4	−6.9	−0.07
No	No, never recognised	1.2	−2.9	−0.27
Total		−2.4	−7.4	−7.4

Note: A closed shop is defined as a situation where management indicated that union membership was conditional on getting or retaining employment (although some firms indicated that they operated a closed shop in name only). In 1993, the question concerned Union Management Agreements, which is defined as a situation where management indicated that union membership was encouraged. Partial derecognition is drawn from answers to the derecognition question in the 1993 survey. N = number of firms, U = unweighted average union density and W = weighted average union density (weights were company employment in 1990, or 1989 if 1990 data not available).

density in other groups. The largest falls in union density within firms occurred where some degree of derecognition took place, especially where derecognition was only partial. Firms who totally derecognised unions had a low density of union membership (33 per cent) to start out with. However, the contribution of derecognising firms to the decline in aggregate union density was modest: some 70 per cent of the total fall in membership occurred in firms where unions were recognised throughout the period.[15] This fall in membership occurred across firms of all sizes, but it was slightly larger among firms with above average employment.[16]

The 1993 survey also asked firms to *indicate the most important level within the organisation (or across a group of companies) at which wage setting occurred*. Table 5.9 gives the breakdown of responses for firms with and without recognised unions. National or multi-company bargains were the most important level of bargaining in only 19 per cent of unionised companies, slightly higher than for non-union companies (11 per cent). For unionised companies, the dominant bargaining level was the individual establishment (38 per cent); amongst non-union companies, individual

Table 5.9 The most important level at which wages are set 1993

Level	Recognised unions		No recognised unions	
	N	%	N	%
National or multi-employer	56	19	34	11
Company but multi-plant	70	24	62	20
By plant but all groups of employees	111	38	39	13
Individuals or separate groups within a plant	44	15	111	36
No response	13	4	65	20

Note: N = number of firms

employee or separate groups of employees within a single plant were the most important decision making unit (36 per cent). Perhaps more interesting are the changes which occurred between 1990 and 1993. National or multi-employer wage-setting agreements declined in importance in 16 per cent of firms with recognised trade unions, while only 2 per cent said they had increased in importance. Company-wide decisions were felt to have declined in importance in 4 per cent of the sample firms and increased in 6 per cent, a pattern also observable with plant level agreements. The most substantial change (although it was only marginally so) was towards individual or group wage setting within a plant: 7 per cent of firms increased and only 3 per cent decreased their bargaining at this level. The contrast between national bargains and the other three groups is the clearest, as, on balance, all the others had net increases in perceived importance. This may reflect increases in the use of individual performance related pay. A similar pattern of net decline in the importance of industry bargains occurred amongst non-union firms (5 per cent of firms reported decreases, while only 2 per cent reported increases), and small net increases were recorded in the other three decision-making levels. In particular, a sharp move towards individual or group wage setting within plants was observed, with some 8 per cent of firms reporting increasing importance and only 1 per cent reporting declines.

Thus, the move towards decentralised pay setting that was evident throughout the 1980s seems to have continued apace.[17] However, as noted earlier, firms have recently begun to make extensive use of temporary wage freezes, with just under 20 per cent of firms having initiated a pay freeze lasting a year or more. Together these changes point to an increase in the ability of managers to set pay without attention to traditional wage relativities across plants/groups within a firm or across firms. Unions appear to have enjoyed only moderate success in resisting this trend. We conjecture that wage outcomes now differ much more across individuals in any establishment and across establishments or enterprises in any sector than in the 1970s or the early to mid-1980s.

These changes are all continuations of trends evident since the 1970s and identifying the extent to which recessionary pressures caused these changes is slightly tricky. Recessions may drive changes in the organisation of employee relations in two quite distinct ways. First, the pressures on firms to reorganise working practices and employee relations are of greater intensity in a recession, and the opportunity costs of making workplace changes are lower when spare capacity exists. This suggests that firms in greater difficulties may take the opportunities available to reduce the reliance on union negotiations to institute changes in wages and work organisation. Alternatively, increased unemployment and the fear of redundancy may reduce the will and ability of workers to resist management initiatives in general. In this case, the recession will influence the decision to reduce union presence irrespective of the intensity of recession induced pressures felt by the firm itself.

To explore these hypotheses, we examined changes in union presence in the 570 firms in our 1993 survey which had indicated how severely the recession had hit their company. Two hundred and ninety-five recognised trade unions, and just under 15 per cent of these firms indicated that they had engaged in partial or total derecognition (12 per cent partial, 3 per cent total). About 12 per cent of the 295 union firms who indicated that they were '*extremely severely*' or '*severely*' hit by the recession engaged in some degree of derecognition, whereas 18 per cent of those who were only '*moderately*' affected and 50 per cent of those who were '*unaffected*' initiated a derecognition. A similar picture emerges from data on plant closures and employment shedding. Union firms which partially or totally derecognised unions reduced the number of plants that they operated by 3.5 per cent (each observation is weighted by the number of plants operated in 1990), whereas union firms with no change in recognition closed nearly 12 per cent. Similarly, derecognising firms shed just under 2 per cent of their 1992 employment (weighted by 1990 employment numbers) while union firms without changes in recognition shed 8 per cent of their labour. These rather surprising numbers suggest that the incidence of recognition was more or less unrelated to either the severity of the impact of the recession, or to the severity of the job shedding response initiated by afflicted firms.

More revealing perhaps are the responses to questions about whether firms had undertaken a reorganisation of working practices, manning levels, or wage payment systems. Table 5.10 shows the responses to these questions according to union status. Union firms were more likely than non-

Table 5.10 *Changes in labour organisation and wage payment systems by union recognition 1990–93*

'Did your company engage in a major overhaul of the following aspects of work organisation in some or all your establishments in the period 1990–1992?'

	No union recognition in 1990	Unions recognised in 1990 no derecognition	Union recognition in 1990 partial derecognition	Unions recognised in 1990 total derecognition
Labour organisation/manning levels/restrictive practices				
Yes, in response to the recession	39%(111)	31%(80)	34%(12)	25%(2)
Yes, but not as a response to the recession	21%(54)	41%(105)	49%(17)	63%(5)
No	31%(89)	21%(54)	17%(6)	0%(0)
No answer	10%(28)	7%(17)	0%(0)	13%(1)
Wage payment systems				
Yes in response to the recession	16%(45)	14%(36)	14%(5)	13%(1)
Yes but not as a response to the recession	21%(61)	33%(85)	43%(15)	63%(5)
No	53%(152)	43%(111)	40%(14)	13%(1)
No answer	10%(30)	9%(24)	3%(1)	13%(1)

union firms to take these actions, but were less likely to do so as a result of recessionary pressures. For firms which derecognised unions, this is even more marked: 51 per cent reorganised their industrial relations system, but not as a result of recessionary pressures (compared with 41 per cent of union firms with unchanged status and 21 per cent of non-union firms). For wage payment systems, 47 per cent of all firms who derecognised unions undertook changes for reasons other than the recession (compared with 33 per cent of union firms with unchanged status and 21 per cent of non-union firms). These changes in organisation are, of course, correlated with changes in union status, but the key insight is that in the eyes of management only a minority were undertaken directly in response to the recession.

Finally, we asked whether the trend toward decentralisation of pay setting could be attributed to the impact of the recession. Defining 'decentralisation' as a firm in which national bargaining declined in importance or local bargaining increased (but ignoring instances where declines in intermediate levels cannot be paired with a increase in importance at a more disaggregated level), it turns out that 108 firms decentralised their bargaining (out of 549 for which the issue is clearly defined). 45 per cent of the firms who decentralised were '*extremely severely*' or '*severely*' affected by the recession. This is the same as the proportion in the population who did not make such a move. It is perhaps unsurprising that decentralisation is strongly correlated with firms reorganising manning arrangements and wage payment systems. However, the proportion of those making reorganisations who replied that these changes were undertaken as a response to the recession was only about 50 per cent, and almost identical in decentralising and non-decentralising firms.

The bottom line, then, is that the recession seems to have had a more substantive impact on decisions to decentralise pay than on union bargaining arrangements or union density. Further, the modest changes which we have observed are as likely as not to have been a continuation of trends long evident in the UK. Although the effects of the 1990–92 recession were transmitted back from the decline in domestic demand to labour markets, almost all of the substantive effects took the form of job shedding. The recession seems to have had only a very modest effect on labour market institutions or industrial relations systems.

Conclusions

Recessions are about cost control, and this means that how a firm operates in the labour market may prove to be a decisive determinant of its ability to withstand recessionary pressures. In practice, this stricture applies to a surprisingly small number of firms who, as it happens, typically make large (and not marginal) changes to stock of employees. Hardly any firms in our sample engaged in cost control without using employment reductions and, more interestingly, it appears that wage growth reductions and employment reductions occurred (for the most part) in the same firms. Further, the extent of employment reduction was not influenced by the additional use of wage restraint even after controlling for the effect of the recession. The primary reason for this is that the impact of wage restraint was marginal given the extreme variation in the desired adjustment of firms. The small number of firms going through large scale changes in employment clearly found the sheer scale of adjustment which they needed to make in the time available to them made wages reductions marginal to the adjustment process. Indeed, over the period studied, the control of wages growth did not noticeably influence employment levels. Since unions affect wages more than employment, they do not seem to have played a major role in affecting how firms have responded to recessionary shocks.

What we have observed in our data is a pattern of behaviour which is more than faintly reminiscent of downsizing; that is, major reductions of employment in a few firms which totally reorganise their operations and re-engineer their processes to reduce head count. Downsizing is not necessarily a recession-induced phenomena, since it is often precipitated by a large gap between how a firm is actually performing and how the capital market thinks it ought to perform, something which can occur during a boom in a poorly managed firm. Downsizing is also frequently accompanied by plant closure and divestiture. It is easy to see all of this in our data but, if recessions differ from booms, it is apparently only in the incidence of downsizing (and then probably only marginally). Perhaps even more surprising is the apparently only very modest role that unions play in shielding their members from the effects of downsizing, whenever it occurs. This may be because downsizing has only become practically possible in the 1980s when union strength began to decline, or it may be that the practices of unions are so heavily bound up with wage bargaining on behalf of members with jobs that they are unable to protect their members' jobs. Either way, it is perhaps no surprise that union membership has fallen, and it is possible that this trend will continue until more substantive changes are made in the role played by unions in corporate decision making processes.

Many economists have speculated that the high rates of job creation and destruction (plus the enhanced flow of workers in and out of unemployment) which we observe is part of a restructuring process. If recessions are periods of accelerated structural change in which firms exploit opportunities created by difficulties facing them or take advantage of temporary falls in the opportunity cost of initiating and carrying out changes, then we should expect to see firms do more than shuffle workers between jobs. In particular, managers out to take advantage of shifts in union-management bargaining power are likely to want to make (or encourage) major changes in their industrial relations practices (amongst other things) which consolidate their temporary advantage. These changes may be many and varied, but the most easily observed manifestations of them include union derecognition, reductions in union membership and shifts to local, plant-level bargaining (possibly coupled with the introduction of individual performance related pay). Our results are only partially consistent with this view. We do observe some of these changes but those that occurred between 1990 and 1992 were fairly modest. Further, the observed changes in union recognition have not occurred primarily in firms that were severely affected by the recession. What is more, increases in pay decentralisation and reorganisation of work practices were as likely to be initiated by distressed firms as they were by firms only moderately affected by the recession. Two conclusions follow from these observations. First, the retreat of UK unionism observed during the 1990–93 recession was, in the main, a continuation of existing (and long-standing) secular trends. The mild acceleration in the pace of change revealed by our survey may be cyclical, but the trend is unlikely to be reversed as recovery gathers pace. Second, while recessions may induce structural changes associated with job reallocation and job restructuring, it is probably unwise to infer from this that they are also a major driver of more important organisational changes or changes in labour market institutions.

Finally, it is clear that many of the shocks to product markets which occur in recessions are transmitted back to labour markets. Although we have not focused on it, the data we examined in Chapter 4 on investment behaviour also suggests that many shocks are transmitted back into intermediate goods markets in the form of abandoned or postponed investments in plant and equipment. However, of the three most important stakeholders of firms—employees, suppliers and shareholders—only the first two seem to bear the brunt of the recession. As we saw in Chapter 4, relatively few firms reduced dividend career, even amongst those who were *extremely seriously* affected. Some have argued that shareholders already bear many risks and, therefore, need to be cushioned from further blows if they are to continue to be willing to invest. However, the capital invested by most shareholders in firms is not sunk (certainly not to the same degree as that of specialised and highly skilled workers or specialist suppliers), and many of their risks can be diversified away (unlike other stakeholders whose fortunes are often tied to those of a single enterprise). Although our data are hardly conclusive, we remain uneasy about just how widely the burdens of recessions are shared amongst those with a stake in badly affected firms.

6   Innovative activity in the recession

Introduction

Economists have long disagreed about what kind of environment provides the right seedbed for stimulating innovative activity. Virtually everyone agrees that innovation should flower where technological opportunities are rich, and many also believe that conditions of appropriability can have an important effect on incentives to innovate. This is not, however, the whole story. Firms must have the internal capabilities to spot, and then exploit, technological opportunities if they are to successfully innovate, something which almost certainly requires them to establish a link between technological possibilities on the one hand and user needs on the other. Further, internal capabilities are also important determinants of spillovers; that is, conditions of appropriability depend, in part, on the information receiving and using abilities of rival firms.

More controversial is the oft heard argument that monopoly power is conducive to innovation. The debate on the Schumpeterian hypothesis has been long and somewhat inconclusive. Many people believe that at least a little bit of competitive adversity is essential to keep firms on their toes, but few subscribe to the view that unbridled competition or extreme adversity stimulates innovation. Although competitive pressures sharpen incentives, they can also limit the ability of firms to innovate. This is particularly the case when firms become too financially pressed to invest in R&D or other complementary forms of investment (like training or marketing) which are necessary to insure the success of an innovation. On the other hand, a lack of competition often breeds complacency, and firms will always be reluctant to introduce innovations which displace rents which they realize from currently profitable activities. Given this diversity of reasonable seeming views, it comes as little surprise to discover that much of the empirical literature gives only (at best) ambiguous support for the Schumpeterian hypothesis. Indeed possibly the clearest conclusion to emerge from the literature is that monopoly power has only a second order effect on innovative activity.[1]

Since recessions have very similar effects on the (residual) demand of firms as increases in competition, it seems natural to think that recessions might be a useful natural experiment to use for assessing the effects that (competitive) adversity has on innovative activity. If, as is widely believed, rent displacement (that is the fear that introducing a new innovation will displace earnings from existing activities) is a major determinant of innovative activity, then there may be a common base between, on the one hand, arguments suggesting that competition (which threatens rents on existing activities) stimulates innovation and arguments which suggest that innovative activity flowers in recession (when existing rent streams dry up). However, the size of many markets shrinks in recessions, and firms may make unduly pessimistic forecasts about future prospects from currently stagnant market circumstances. Both of these effects should work to inhibit innovation, particularly if innovative activity is very sensitive to conditions of demand. Thus, one of our goals in what follows is to explore the interrelated questions of how adversity affects innovative activity, and whether recessions are a time of heightened innovative activity.

Examining what happens to innovative activity in recessions is interesting for a second reason. It is widely accepted that productivity growth rates vary procyclically, meaning that productivity rises as recessions end.[2] This, in turn, suggests that whatever it is which stimulates cyclically driven productivity growth surges may occur during the preceding recession. Clearly, labour shedding, the closure of inefficient old plants and their replacement by more efficient new plants, changes in organisational structures and shopfloor and/or managerial processes are all likely to induce at least a transitory increase in productivity.[3] However, if recessions are seedbeds of innovative activity, then this should stimulate productivity. What is more, if recessions unleash a 'gale of creative destruction' which creates new markets and stimulates demand, then innovative activity may also be responsible (at least in part) for bringing recessions to an end, and ushering in the next boom. One of our goals in this chapter, then, is to look at the relationship between changes in demand—and, more specifically, between the transition from slump to boom—and innovative activity, looking at whether innovative activity might be a prime determinant of both the timing of cyclical upturns and/or the productivity growth spurt which accompanies them.

As we have seen, recessions have relatively selective effects on firms and a surprisingly large number of firms bring forward investments in new products and processes. This raises two interesting questions. First, innovation is often described as a coupling process which combines R&D or technological knowledge with engineering or manufacturing expertise and knowledge about user needs. If this is true, firms who bring forward new product or process innovations are likely to make a range of complementary investments, and it would be interesting to identify what these are. Second, not all firms bring forward innovative activity in recessions, and it is interesting to ask who these innovative firms are and to speculate on what prompts them to act when other firms do not. Amongst other things, arguments about the stimulating effects of competitive adversity suggest that these firms may be drawn disproportionately from the ranks of those who were *extremely severely* affected by the recession or who expected that it would last well beyond the Spring of 1993. This is a hypothesis which our data ought to be informative on.

The plan is as follows. We review first some of the literature on how demand affects innovative activity to help set the stage for what follows. Most of the work reported in this literature, however, focuses only on innovative output (by and large), and does not provide much information on how demand affects decisions to invest in R&D or to implement new product/process development. Our data enables us to examine how these decisions are affected by recessionary pressures. The complicating feature of these exercises is that innovative activity can, and should, encompass many things. Investments in the development of new products or new processes often require complementary investments in R&D, marketing, plant and equipment, training and so on. It is, therefore, important to examine a number of different investment decisions, and explore the complementarities which exist between them. This we do in the third section, again using data derived from our survey. This leads naturally to a final set of exercises, namely that of identifying innovative firms. This is the subject of the final section, which utilises probit models to identify firms who bring forward product and process innovations, or who bring forward R&D expenditures, training or advertising and marketing.

Adversity and decisions to innovate

Most economists distinguish supply-push influences on innovation from demand-pull influences and, for many, the proposition that market conditions affect decisions to innovate quickly reduces itself to the hypothesis that demand matters. Supply-push summarises a range of determinants of innovative activities, including the evolution of scientific knowledge, the productivity of research labs, the conversion of scientific principles into widely understood and easy to use engineering technology, and so on. Although many of these forces are affected by the state of the economy and decisions made by particular firms in the medium to long run, it is hard to believe that they are profoundly affected by cyclical fluctuations in economic activity or that they are endogeneous to the short-run operating decisions of most firms. By contrast, demand-pull influences on innovative activity include a range of effects driven by changes in tastes, incomes, relative prices, the competitive structure of markets, conditions of appropriability and expectations of future prices, incomes and technological developments. Although it is hard to believe that chains of feedback between decisions to innovate and market outcomes operate very rapidly, it is nevertheless the case that innovative activity is likely to be cyclical in nature if demand pull factors matter.

To make progress in assessing the relative roles of supply-push and demand-pull, it is useful to make a distinction between the invention and the implementation of new innovations. Invention describes the development of new scientific principles and their translation into new technologies. Although invention decisions can often be influenced by the expectations that potential inventing firms have about market opportunities, there is a wealth of circumstantial evidence which suggests that the constraints imposed on the process of invention by incomplete scientific knowledge and lack of expertise are important.[4] For this reason, it seems natural to believe that invention is primarily driven by supply-push forces. When, however, an invention occurs, firms often have a choice about when they embody it in a new product or process and introduce it on to the market. Such implementation decisions are obviously market based and, if firms actually have some latitude in making implementation decisions, then the development of new products or processes will not necessarily be closely timed with their invention. This gap between invention and implementation creates a window of opportunity for demand-pull forces to affect innovative activity.

The question that remains is to ascertain whether demand-pull effects on implementation decisions (if they exist) generate counter- or procyclical variations in innovative activity. The argument that innovative activity is countercyclical largely turns on the opportunity costs of innovation. One source of opportunity costs is those which arise when a firm transforms its internal structure and operations to accommodate a new production process or the marketing of a new product. Since such transformations often require substantial time inputs from senior managers who also have operational responsibilities, one source of opportunity costs is the time such managers would otherwise have spent managing current operations. Current activities are likely to be much less profitable in recessions and, as a consequence, the costs of implementing new innovations will also be lower in recessions.[5] Another component of opportunity costs is displaced rents.[6] Established firms generate rents from their existing producing and selling activities, and new products or processes which are substitutes for these activities displace existing rents and, *ceteris paribus*, raise the costs of implementation. However, since existing rents are likely to fall during a recession, the disincentive they create to implement new inventions also weakens. The result is likely to be an increase in the implementation of new inventions.

By contrast, at least two arguments have been advanced which suggest that innovative activity may be procyclical. The first focuses on the limited ability of markets to absorb new products. Each new product or process implemented at any particular time competes with a range of existing products, and each is likely to be followed by imitators who intensify that competition. As more and more new products come on to the market at any one time, competition for consumer spending reduces the likely profitability of each and this, in turn, will reduce the incentive to innovate. The implementation of new inventions is likely to resume when economic growth generates enough market expansion to absorb more new products. Indeed, the expectation of further market growth is likely to stimulate a wave of implementation decisions geared to taking advantage of the expansion in demand. This suggests that implementation decisions are likely to be timed at the end of recession, and will be led by firms who expect an imminent cyclical upturn. The second argument which suggests that implementation decisions will be procyclical starts from the observation that appropriability problems mean that inventors will only have a limited window of opportunity in which to generate profits from their innovative activities. As a consequence, they will wish to implement their inventions during a period of time when they are likely to earn most profits. This is, of course, likely to be during periods of high and growing demand. Indeed, if what drives these decisions are expectations of future demand growth (rather than actual current rates of growth), then, if all firms hold similar expectations and act on them, waves of innovative activity are likely to precede and, in so doing, cause increases in demand.[7]

Most of the early evidence consistent with the view that increases in demand stimulate innovative activity was produced by Schmookler. He observed spurts of patenting activity by intermediate goods manufacturers following increases in demand for the capital goods they produced. A number of subsequent cross-section studies have uncovered positive but

········· Patents – – – – – Index of Manufacturing Output ———— Innovations

Figure 6.1 *Innovations and patents in the UK 1948–88*

fairly weak (and often imprecisely measured) effects of demand on measures of R&D spending, counts of patents, or counts of major innovations produced.[8] Although there is not much time-series evidence available to compute correlations and assess causal patterns between demand and innovative activity, what little we do have suggests that the two are positively correlated and that increases in demand lead changes in innovative activity. Figure 6.1 shows the basic data from a recent time-series study of the innovations and patents produced by manufacturing firms in the UK over the period 1948–93 plotted against an index of manufacturing output. Even without using sophisticated statistical techniques, it is fairly clear that the production of major innovations and patents is procyclical, rising and falling as GDP rises and falls. The important relationship seems to be between the level of innovative activity (however measured) and manufacturing output, although much of the greater volatility in the level of innovative activity over time means that the elasticity of innovative activity with respect to output is hard to estimate with precision. It is also much harder to see a pattern between changes in output on levels of innovative activity or between changes in output and changes in innovative activity simply by inspection. In fact, more formal testing using an error correction model reveals that the important relationship in the data is a fairly robust long-run positive correlation between innovative activity and the level of demand. It also is the case that the production of major innovations are more sensitive to demand than patents and that demand (Granger) causes changes in patents, and innovations but not *vice versa*.[9]

Table 6.1 The effect of the recession on investment behaviour

	Plant/machinery	R&D	Product innovation	Process innovation	Training	Advertising/marketing	Buildings
No of firms who abandoned or postponed investments in	275	117	65	78	161	197	245
No of firms who brought forward investments in	81	116	200	155	180	132	57%
% of those who abandoned/postponed investments who were 'extremely severely' affected	25%	30%	29%	26%	26%	27%	26%
% of those who brought forward investments who were 'extremely severely' affected	14%	7.8%	16%	13%	12%	16%	7%
% of those who abandoned or postponed investments who thought that the recession was over	4%	3%	3%	6%	6%	8%	4%
% of those who abandoned/postponed investments who thought that the recession would last 12+ months	53%	55%	58%	56%	53%	50%	57%
% of those who brought forward investments who thought that the recession was over	49%	42%	50%	47%	49%	53%	40%
% of those who brought forward investments who thought that the recession would last 12+ months	16%	13%	9%	8%	11%	8%	30%

Although examining variations in the production of major innovations and patents across the economy as a whole over time is an interesting exercise, to make much progress in exploring the effects that adversity has on decisions to invent or to implement new inventions one needs to focus more directly on the actions taken by individual firms. In Chapter 4, we examined the investment decisions made by the firms in our sample, and Table 6.1 reproduces some of the material displayed in Tables 4.7 and 4.8 in a slightly different form. As we saw earlier, investments in plant and machinery and investments in buildings were badly affected by the recession, with 275 firms postponing or abandoning their investment plans whilst only 81 brought them forward. Investments in R&D and marketing were also more frequently abandoned or postponed than they were brought forward. However, investments in training, product innovation and process innovation were much less likely to be abandoned or postponed than the other four types of investment shown on the table. Further, three times as many firms brought forward product innovations as postponed or abandoned them, twice as many brought forward process innovations and more brought forward investments in training than abandoned or postponed them.

It is also possible to work out how many firms took no action whatsoever to alter their investment plans from Table 6.1 (for each column, subtract the sum down the first two rows from 586). The striking thing about this calculation is that 61 per cent of firms in our sample did not alter their plans to invest in process innovation, 60 per cent of firms did not alter their R&D investment plans, 51 per cent did not alter their product innovation plans. The differences between decisions to invest in R&D or in new product/process innovation on the one hand, and other investment decisions is fairly substantial. Only 44 per cent of the firms in our sample chose not to alter their marketing plans, 42 per cent chose not to alter training plans and 39 per cent did not alter plant and equipment investment plans. As noted earlier, this in part reflects selectivity in the effects of recessions on firms. However, it is also clearly noticeable that the effects of recessionary pressures on investments in R&D and innovation are much weaker than they are on investment in plant and machinery, an observation entirely consistent with the much weaker effects that demand variables exhibit in econometric studies of innovation than in studies of investment in plant and machinery. Investments in marketing and training fall in between these extremes: they are more sensitive to cyclical pressures than investments in implementing product or process innovations, but less sensitive than investments in plant and equipment. As we noted in Chapter 4, the net effect is that the ratio of investment in intangibles to investment in tangibles varies countercyclically.[10]

If, as seems reasonable, investments in plant and in buildings require a lot of cash, then these results may reflect the effects of financial constraints on firms investments behavior. Firms with cash flow problems, particularly those who are *extremely seriously* affected by the recession, are likely to have been forced to cut back on big ticket investment expenditure programmes but may be able to spend on smaller projects (particularly those which help to prop up sagging activities in existing markets). Following 'pit-stop' theorists, one might push this argument one step further, however, and argue that investments in various intangibles like R&D and innovation use senior management time more intensively than others and are, therefore, brought forward in recessions when the opportunity cost of that time is low.[11] Although this argument has a certain attractiveness, it is hard to believe that investments in marketing, training or R&D are more demanding of senior management time than investments in plant. The kind of investment activity which is both management time intensive and not too demanding in terms of cash flow is organisational change and, as we have seen, the extent to which this occurs in recessions is limited. One concludes, then, that the data on Table 6.1 may be most easily accounted for by the hypothesis of cash constraints.

The third and fourth rows of Table 6.1 show the investment decisions of firms who were *extremely severely* affected by the recession. Roughly speaking, between 25 and 30 per cent of firms who abandoned or postponed any of the seven types of investments shown on the table were *extremely severely* affected by the recession. Since only 18 per cent of the whole sample of responding firms reported themselves as being *extremely severely* affected by the recession and between 40 and 60 per cent of all respondents to the survey did not alter their investment plans, these figures suggest that a surprisingly large number of *extremely severely* affected firms did not abandon or postpone investments in plant, R&D, marketing, training, and so on. On the other hand, quite a number of firms who were not *extremely severely* affected abandoned or postponed one or more of these seven types of investment. Further, the fourth row of the table shows that between 7 and 16 per cent of *extremely severely* affected firms actually brought forward investments of different types.

One way to interpret these results is to argue that they mean that current market conditions have only a modest effect on investment decisions. This argument would be easier to accept if, at the same time, it could be shown that current expectations of future market conditions had a substantive impact on investment decisions. The bottom four columns on Table 6.1 show how decisions to abandon/postpone or bring forward various types of investments were affected by expectations about the likely length of the recession. Many more firms who thought that the recession was over brought forward than abandoned or postponed investments, and of those firms who abandoned or postponed investments, between 6 and 14 times as many firms thought that the recession would last at least 12 more months as thought that it was over. Similarly, many more of the firms who thought that the recession would last twelve or more months abandoned or postponed investments than brought them forward, and between 3 and 7 times as many of the firms who brought forward investments thought that the recession was over as thought that it would last for at least another year. All of this is at least roughly consistent with the view that expectations about future market conditions matter. Further, since current expectations about the future seem to be a more discriminating predictor of which firms brought forward or abandoned/postponed investments than many of the obvious financial measures of current period performance, one is tempted to conclude that expectations may matter more than current market conditions in affecting investment. This observation seems to apply equally to all seven of the types of investment shown on the table.

It is worth recalling that the data on Table 6.1 refer to investment plans, and needs to be interpreted in the light of the other actions which firms took. In particular, many of the *'extremely severely'* affected firms in our sample closed plants and shed labour, actions which involve actual disinvestment rather than cutting back on planned investment. That is, the total scale back in investment in physical, human and other forms of intangible capital made by *'extremely severely'* affected firms includes both the reduction in desired levels of capital shown on Table 6.1 as well as the reduction in actual capital stock embodied in plant and labour. Thus, it is entirely possible that even firms who brought forward investment in plant and equipment emerged from the recession with a reduced stock of physical capital. Curiously the one area where this might not be quite so obviously the case is product innovation, since the stock of such innovations maintained by firms is often reflected in the breadth of their product line. As we saw in Chapter 4, relatively few firms rationalised their product lines in the recession, suggesting that new product innovators may well have expanded the scope of their market activities.

In sum, all of the data that we have examined is consistent with the (very plausible) *a priori* view that demand has at least a modest effect in stimulating the production of patents and major innovations (although its effects on R&D spending decisions are a little less clear). This may be more true for demand in the sense of current expectations about future market prospects than demand in the sense of current market conditions. Innovative activity seems to be tied to the level of economic activity (but only rather roughly), rising as economies emerge from recessions and falling with decreases in demand. There is no strong evidence suggesting that innovative activity stimulates demand, and most firms who bring forward innovations in recessions seem to do so because they think the recession has ended. Recessions are not, it seems, a seedbed for implementing innovations, and it is not even clear that they stimulate much inventive activity.[12]

Interrelationships between types of investment

It is clear that firms do not make decisions on one type of investment independently of the decisions they make on other types of investment. Most factors of production are either substitutes or complements to each other and, indeed, at least part of the reason for organising production in large establishments is the superior efficiency of teams in carrying certain tasks. Economists are used to thinking of factors of production as being substitutes for each other, a view which is grounded in observations of traditional mass production systems where capital and unskilled labour are typically substitutes for each other. However, many of the new flexible production technologies using a variety of IT systems and multiskilled operatives create complementarities between inputs, and creating corporate competencies requires firms to combine machinery, knowledge capital, and human capital of various types in a complementary fashion to effect some end.[13] If this is truly the case, then one expects to see cross correlations between the various types of investment decision shown on Table 6.1, and it would be interesting to identify which types of investment activity are most strongly correlated with each other, and whether they are substitutes or complements.

Innovation, for example, is likely to be a complementarity generating competence, since it couples technological (and, sometimes, scientific) knowledge with marketing knowledge about user needs and production knowledge about efficient manufacturing to produce new products or processes. In particular, since the success of new products depends on the creation of markets for them, it seems reasonable to believe that investments in product innovation and marketing are likely to be highly correlated.[14] Further, new products often require new production processes and new skills, suggesting that product and process innovations ought to be highly correlated with each other, and with training decisions. Similarly, process innovations often demand new production skills and are, therefore, likely to induce added investments in training. On the other hand, new processes often require new forms of capital equipment (as may some new products),

Table 6.2 The number of firms which brought forward investments

	Plant/ machinery	Building	R&D	Product innovation	Process innovation	Training	Advert-ising
Plant/machinery	–						
Building	32	–					
R&D	37	30	–				
Product innovation	45	32	101	–			
Process innovation	37	26	79	119	–		
Training	47	35	66	98	91	–	
Advertising	34	28	46	73	55	75	–
Total	81	57	116	200	155	180	132

but one expects that firms will have strong incentives to introduce only those new products and processes during a recession which do not require extensive (and very expensive) investments in plant. Further, it is not entirely clear that investments in R&D and investment in new products or processes will be highly correlated. There are often long lags between the discovery of new scientific knowledge and its embodiment in new products or processes and, in any case, new products or processes do not always emerge from R&D labs. In short, it seems reasonable to believe that investments in new product or process innovations are likely to be positively correlated with investments in training and marketing, but that complementarities with investment in plant will be much weaker in recessions.

The data displayed on Tables 6.2 and 6.3 suggest that some of these speculations are at least roughly consistent with the data. Table 6.2 shows that firms who brought forward new product innovations tended also to bring forward new process innovations (56 per cent did), investments in R&D (50 per cent) and investments in training (47 per cent), but that they rarely brought forward investments in plant and machinery (22 per cent), advertising and marketing (34 per cent) or buildings (16 per cent). Those firms who brought forward new process innovations tended also to bring forward product innovations (77 per cent) and investments in both training (58 per cent) and R&D (50 per cent), but very few of them brought forward investments in plant and equipment (25 per cent) or advertising and marketing (35 per cent). In both cases, new innovations seemed to be much more complementary with investments in training than they were with investments in advertising and marketing. The weak correlation

Table 6.3 *The number of firms which abandoned or postponed investments*

	Plant/ machinery	Building	R&D	Product innovation	Process innovation	Training	Advert- ising
Plant/machinery	–						
Building	179	–					
R&D	99	86	–				
Product innovation	53	42	52	–			
Process innovation	65	54	60	42	–		
Training	122	96	71	39	55	–	
Advertising	132	120	74	46	50	105	–
Total	275	245	117	65	78	161	197

between innovation and marketing is a surprise which is difficult to account for, particularly since one expects to see a stronger correlation between new product innovation and marketing than between new process innovations and marketing. Studies of *successful* innovation often associate success with a successful coupling between technology and user needs, and the weak link we observe in our data between these two types of investment may indicate that a number of these new product innovations are destined to fail. Alternately, investments in training may refer to training sales people, something which might reasonably be described as an investment in marketing.

Table 7.3 shows that much the same considerations apply to decisions to abandon or postpone different types of investment. Firms that cut investments in product innovation also tended to drop process innovations (65 per cent) and *vice versa* (54 per cent), and both were more likely to cut R&D (80 per cent and 77 per cent respectively) than training (60 per cent and 71 per cent) or advertising and marketing (71 per cent and 64 per cent). Training and advertising investments tended to be cut together: 65 per cent of firms who cut training also cut advertising and marketing, while 53 per cent of those who cut advertising and marketing also cut training. Firms who cut R&D investments also tended to cut advertising and marketing (63 per cent) and training (61 per cent).

In fact, the complementarities involving new product and process innovation seem to be the strongest which exist in the data. Investments in innovation are more complementary with other forms of investment than are, for example, investments in R&D or in plant and machinery. What is, perhaps, more surprising is the weak complementarity between investments in innovation and investments in R&D. One hundred and seventeen firms abandoned or postponed investments in R&D, 78 in process innovations and 65 product innovations, but only 146 firms did one or more of these

Table 6.4 Other actions taken by firms which brought forward investments

	Product & process innovations	R&D	Training	Advert- ising/ marketing	Plant/ machinery	All firms
% who reduce dividends	31	31	30	32	25	35
% who develop overseas markets	71	71	61	56	68	52
% who close establishments	57	56	59	51	44	56
% who reduce employment	55	47	47	48	44	49
% who reduce HQ costs	73	75	72	78	63	72
% who focus	57	55	57	60	56	54
% with new CEO	22	29	29	23	21	26
% who changed their organisational structure	70	65	70	68	64	65
% who recognised unions	55	48	51	46	60	48

Note: This is an answer to the question, #5 in Section I of the survey, and the numbers in the table refer to firms who thought that the 'action (was) very necessary' or 'action taken and of some importance'.

and only 40 firms did all three. Similarly, 200 firms brought forward product innovations, 155 brought forward process innovations and 116 brought forward investments in R&D, but only 244 firms did one or more of these and only 72 did all three. It is important not to read too much into these numbers. Innovative activity is undoubtedly related to investments in R&D, but not all innovations originate in a scientific laboratory, and current R&D spending is not always a good measure of the stock of a firm's R&D capital.

Table 6.4 shows the complementarities which appear in the data between decisions to bring forward various types of investment and the other strategic decisions made in response to recessionary pressures discussed earlier in Chapter 4. Firms who brought forward investments in product and process innovations, R&D, training, advertising and marketing and plant and machinery appear to differ relatively little amongst themselves with respect to the other strategic choices which they made. The two exceptions to this are, first, that firms who brought forward investments in plant and machinery were much less likely to reduce dividends, close establishments and reduce headquarters costs than other firms. Second, firms that brought forward product and process innovations were more likely than most other firms to develop overseas markets, reduce employment and change their organisational structure. This said, it seems clear from the table that there do not appear to be strong complementarities between the strategic actions

firms took in response to recessionary pressures and their investment behaviour. Since most of the strategic responses which firms made to
recessionary pressures were related to cutting costs by closing plants and
shedding jobs, this is not surprising.

Perhaps the clearest feature of Tables 6.2 and 6.3 is the observation that
product and process innovation tends to proceed hand in hand, and these
two interrelated investment decisions appear to be the source of many of
the most marked complementarities between different types of investments
thrown up in the data. Since product and process innovation seems to be
so highly complementary, and since one or (usually) both are more frequently brought forward in recessions than other types of investment, it is
worth concentrating our attention on the firms who choose to accelerate
their investments in both new product and new process innovations in the
recession.

There are 119 innovative firms in our sample who brought forward investments in both product and process innovations. Seventy-two of them
(61 per cent) also brought forward investments in R&D and 71 (60 per
cent) brought forward investments in training, but only 47 (39 per cent)
brought forward investments in advertising and marketing and only 28 (25
per cent) brought forward investments in plant and machinery.[15] These
numbers are qualitatively similar but quantitatively larger than those for
all firms, much as one might expect. Possibly more interestingly, only 19
of these firms (16 per cent) did nothing but bring forward investments in
product and process innovations; that is, 84 per cent of the innovating firms
in our sample also brought forward some other form of investment. That
is, the data suggest that the firms who actively pursued new product or
process innovation strategies in recessions were actually pursuing a broader
based investment strategy which usually also involved investments in R&D
and training, but only sometimes included investments in marketing or in
plant. This same observation emerges if one cuts the data in a slightly different way. Only 21 of the innovative firms who brought forward product
and process innovations abandoned or postponed investments in R&D, 33
abandoned or postponed investments in training and 45 abandoned or
postponed investments in marketing. Sixty-five (that is 55 per cent) did,
however, abandon or postpone investments in plant and equipment. Conversely, of the 42 firms who abandoned or postponed investments in new
products and processes, only 1 brought forward investments in R&D, 10
brought forward training investments, 8 brought forward marketing investments and 1 brought forward investments in plant and equipment. One
way or the other, these 119 innovative firms seem to stand out in the data,
and identifying who they are is the next task.

Table 6.5 The characteristics of firms which brought forward investments

	Product & process innovations	R&D	Training	Advert- ising/ marketing	Plant/ machinery	All firms
Profit margin, 1989	12.8	13.1	13.9	12.9	13.8	14.4
Change in margins, 1986–89	00.4	1.0	0.9	1.6	3.3	1.2
Log employment, 1989	7.15	7.00	7.01	6.77	7.01	6.80
Growth of sales, 1984–9	49.7	56.8	54.4	51.9	51.3	52.9
Cash/liabilities, 1989	19.8	21.6	16.8	17.7	18.9	19.7
Debt/assets, 1989	18.2	15.9	16.8	18.0	14.7	18.1
% holding companies	30	35	30	30	32	34
% functionally organised	29	28	34	36	32	32
% divisionalised	37	31	32	32	35	29
% foreign owned	19	20	21	20	20	17
% highly dispersed	41	34	38	27	32	37
% 2+ acquisitions	26	24	21	20	21	25
Export as a of sales	23.4	24.8	21.4	16.8	21.5	17.0

Identifying innovative firms

Innovative firms are those which have rich investment opportunities and confident expectations about the future. As we have seen, most of the firms in our sample who brought forward product or process innovations were not '*extremely severely*' affected by the recession, and many of them were fairly confident (in the Spring of 1993) that the recession was nearly over. To argue that innovative firms are those with both the opportunity and the inclination to innovate does not, however, say much, for investment opportunities must be created and expectations are as likely to reflect a firm's ability to cope with its environment as they are a reflection of the future shape of that environment. To identify innovative firms, then, it is necessary to identify the attributes of firms which are able to act in circumstances which inhibit most of their rivals or peers.

Table 6.5 identifies a number of the characteristics of the firms who brought forward various types of investments. The 119 innovators are in the first column, and, to facilitate comparisons, those who brought forward investments in R&D in the second, and so on. What stands out most is that innovators were larger, slightly more likely to be divisionalised, had a

Table 6.6 *The characteristics of firms which postponed or abandoned invest-ments*

	Product & process innovations	R&D	Training	Advert-ising/ marketing	Plant/ machinery
Profit margin, 1989	0.109	0.118	0.115	0.132	0.127
Change in margins, 1986–9	−0.019	−0.007	−0.007	−0.002	0.006
Log employment, 1989	6.63	6.76	6.52	6.66	6.76
Growth of sales, 1984–9	0.676	0.557	0.558	0.592	0.541
Cash/liabilities, 1989	0.144	0.141	0.170	0.180	0.173
Debt/assets, 1989	0.195	0.198	0.181	0.180	0.177
% holding companies	31	32	37	40	35
% functionally organised	31	32	33	28	31
% divisionalised	31	31	26	26	31
% foreign owed	12	15	15	14	16
% highly dispersed	38	39	34	40	38
% 2+ acquisitions	31	26	27	31	27
Export as % of sales	14.4	16.2	14.4	16.1	15.9

slightly more dispersed ownership structure and were more export oriented than others. They were, however, a little less profitable than other firms prior to the recession, they experienced weaker profits and sales growth, and had higher debt. However, only size, divisionalisation, and shareholder dispersion clearly mark innovators out from all other firms. Firms that brought forward R&D had relatively low debt, high growth and were rela-tively cash rich and export oriented. By contrast, firms who brought forward training were profitable, fast growing, cash poor, divisionalised, foreign owned and export oriented. Marketing active firms were unusu-ally small, had less cash, higher ownership structures and they were domestically oriented. Not surprisingly, firms that brought forward invest-ments in plant had low debt, relatively high profiles, were divisionalised but with relatively low ownership dispersion and they were somewhat less acquisition oriented. What is not immediately evident from Table 6.5 is the (surprising) fact that firms who did not change their investment plans were the most profitable of all.

To put Table 6.5 into some perspective, Table 6.6 shows the character-istics of firms who postponed or abandoned various types of investments. Unsurprisingly, these firms were, in general, less profitable than others and they had experienced profit declines prior to the recession. They often car-ried higher levels of debt (and less cash), were smaller and had grown more rapidly prior to the recession. Needless to say, these are all characteristics which we have found (in Chapter 3) to be associated with the probability that a firm was 'extremely severely' affected by the recession.

The question of what makes a firm innovative is an old one, and has never been satisfactorily resolved. Economists have produced a number of correlations between the incidence of innovative activity across firms measured in various ways, and observable characteristics of firms like size and market share. These correlations can be imprecise and unstable at times, and they do not help to explain the episodic nature of innovative activity or patenting.[16] They also do not tell us much about what it is that makes a firm innovative. The popular literature has produced a range of suggestions (usually more prescriptive than descriptive) which often involve creating cross-functional teams, allowing scientists scope to follow their interests, and using performance measures which directly reflect innovative activity, but none of it provides much guide to how one might go about specifying an econometric model designed to answer this question.

Easily the simplest model which one might use builds on the notion that firms innovate whenever they can, and adds a second, much stronger hypothesis, namely that the main determinant of this is the state of their current trading performance. In the context of this study, this suggests that the extent to which firms were 'extremely severely' affected by the recession is (or should be) the driving determinant of whether a firm was an innovator, or, more generally, whether it brought forward any type of investment in the recession. This seems to be a fairly interesting null hypothesis, and we will set it against the alternative that any or all of the observables used on Tables 6.5 and 6.6 make an independent contribution to recessionary pressures. None of these variables takes us very far into examining any of the many propositions generated in the popular sense on innovativeness, and past econometric work suggests that firm size and, perhaps, cash flow and growth are the characteristics most likely to be associated with innovativeness.

In fact, it turns out that virtually none of the characteristics of firms shown on Tables 6.5 and 6.6 matter once the severity of impact of the recession is taken into account. We ran a large number of probit regressions designed to identify firms who postponed or abandoned product or process innovations, R&D, training and advertising and marketing, and they all produced pretty much the same result: the severity of the impact of the recession was the driving force behind the abandoning or postponement of any of these investments. Further, after controlling for the effect of the recession, no other systematic story can be told about firms abandoning or postponing investments (not even industry dummies mattered). Identi-

Table 6.7 *Identifying innovative firms*

	Probability that the firm brought forward			
	Prod. and process innovation	R&D	Training	Marketing
Profit margin, 1989	−0.291	−0.439	0.194	−0.984
	(0.609)	(0.634)	(0.566)	(0.617)
Change in margins	−0.982	−0.087	−0.444	1.04
	(0.881)	(0.913)	(0.825)	(0.841)
Log employment	0.055	0.074	0.066	−0.007
	(0.044)	(0.046)	(0.041)	(0.044)
Growth of sales	−0.037	0.141	0.183	0.011
	(0.1285)	(0.125)	(0.115)	(0.118)
Cash/liabilities	−0.029	0.029	−0.604	−0.604
	(0.248)	(0.252)	(0.250)	(0.241)
Debt/assets	0.041	−0.342	−0.618	0.164
	(0.355)	(0.395)	(0.356)	(0.354)
Exports	0.007	0.010	0.007	−0.0007
	(0.003)	(0.003)	(0.003)	(0.002)
Ownership highly dispersed	−0.031	−0.088	−0.208	−0.137
	(0.134)	(0.135)	(0.123)	(0.128)
Holding company	−0.122	0.128	−0.172	−0.191
	(0.140)	(0.140)	(0.130)	(0.137)
2+ acquisitions	0.057	−0.077	−0.222	−0.191
	(0.158)	(0.160)	(0.146)	(0.156)
Union recognised	−0.018	−0.150	−0.018	−0.089
	(0.147)	(0.150)	(0.135)	(0.143)
Extremely severely affected	−0.480	−0.543	−0.374	−0.202
	(0.212)	(0.221)	(0.181)	(0.189)
Severely affected	−0.003	0.035	−0.194	−0.052
	(0.144)	(0.146)	(0.136)	(0.144)
Recession over 6–12m	0.209	0.056	0.008	0.305
	(0.194)	(0.193)	(0.181)	(0.203)
Recession over 12+m	0.148	0.023	0.144	0.425
	(0.193)	(0.190)	(0.175)	(0.198)
Number of obs.	520	520	520	520
Pseudo R²	0.042	0.053	0.051	0.028

Note: All equations include a constant; standard errors are given in brackets below the estimated coefficients.

fying who brought forward various types of investment was slightly easier, and Table 6.7 shows a sample of the regressions that we ran. Innovative firms were clearly more likely to be export oriented than not, and they were also significantly less likely to have been 'extremely severely' affected by the recession than non-innovators. Those are, however, the only two characteristics significantly associated with the probability that a firm brought forward new product and process innovations. These two characteristics were also associated with the probability that a firm brought forward R&D and training investments. R&D and training were also positively (but not quite significantly) associated with rapid prerecession growth and large size. Training was (puzzlingly) less likely to be brought forward by cash rich, high debt and very acquisitive firms. Marketing investments were the only ones of the four shown on the table to be affected by expectations about the future of the recession, and these correlations suggest (perversely) that firms who were less likely to agree that the recession was over were more likely to bring forward advertising and marketing expenditures. At the end of the day, however, the evidence against the null hypothesis that only the severity of the impact of the recession matters in explaining innovativeness or, more generally, investment behaviour, is not impressive enough to reject that null.

The bottom line seems to be that firms bring forward new product and process investments or other types of investments when they think that the recession is over. The firms that do this are those which have proved not to be vulnerable to recessionary pressures. Almost every other observable characteristic of these firms affects innovativeness or investment behaviour only because they are associated with vulnerability. Two observations follow from this conclusion. First, since it is rather difficult to predict which firms are likely to be vulnerable to recessions (see Chapter 3 above), it follows that predicting which firms are likely to be innovative at any particular time will also be rather difficult. Second, since innovative firms are those who are not badly affected by the recession and think that it is over, it is hard to argue that the innovative activity which occurs in recessions precedes (much less causes) the recovery in output which signals the end of the recession. This is consistent with the time-series evidence we examined at the beginning of the chapter and, taken together, the two observations cast doubt on supply or innovation led stories of the onset of booms. Innovative activity follows demand, and those innovations which are introduced in recessions are not the product of extreme adversity so much as they are a reflection of the fact that many firms are not severely affected by recessions.

Conclusions

Many economists believe that competitive adversity increases the incentives of economic agents to act boldly and take risks. Although the application of these arguments to innovative activity is rather more controversial than their application to, say, actions designed to control costs, enough people still believe that competitive adversity stimulates innovation to make it worth empirical study. Recessions are an interesting 'natural experiment' to use in this context, not least because many of the effects of recessions are similar to those faced by firms operating in markets that have suddenly become more competitive. Further, many of the hypotheses associating competition and incentives to innovate have analogues linking market conditions in recessions to innovative activity.

The evidence which we have examined is not consistent with the view that recessions stimulate innovative activity. The time-series data on innovative output displayed in Figure 6.1 shows that increases in output predate increases in the production of major innovations and patents, while the data generated by our survey on decisions to invest in R&D, product and process innovation indicates that firms who bring forward such activities have not been 'extremely severely' affected by the recession and/or think that it is over. It is hard to see in this any support for views that fluctuations in real output are driven by technology shocks; nor is there any obvious reason to think that an economy needs to go into recession from time to time in order to release its latent innovative energies.[17]

Innovative firms seem to (more or less) randomly select themselves from the sub-set of the population of firms who are not 'extremely severely' affected by the recession and are of the view that the recession is over. Whoever they are, it is clear that they tend to undertake a range of complementary investments simultaneously. Many of them bring forward investments in training and, less clearly, R&D; rather fewer of them also bring forward investments in advertising and marketing or in plant and equipment. Indeed, one of the interesting (and, for us, unexpected) features of recessions is the shifting balance between different types of investment. Part of this seems to arise because investments in new product or process innovations are much less sensitive to changes in market conditions than are investments in plant and equipment or, slightly less clearly, in advertising and marketing. Although this pattern may reflect the opportunity costs of making different types of investments in recessions, it seems more likely that cash or other financial constraints are the real drivers of countercyclical movements in the ratio of investment in intangibles to investment in tangibles. Part of it also certainly arises because successful innovative activity typically couples together a range of skills, including technological knowledge, manufacturing know-how and knowledge about user needs. As a consequence, firms that find opportunities to bring forward product or process innovations as recessions come to a close are also likely to bring forward investment training and, slightly less clearly, R&D, advertising and marketing and plant. Perhaps strongest of all, however, are the complementarities between bringing forward new product innovations and new process innovations.

There are a number of explanations of why productivity growth rates tend to increase during cyclical upswings current in the literature, and there is no strong reason in our data for believing that the increases in innovative activity which occur as economies emerge from recessions are not a potentially important part of the story. If this innovative activity really does stimulate productivity growth, it is not just because of the new products or process innovations themselves. As we have seen, these investments are highly complementary with training and, to a lesser extent, R&D. Such activities are quite likely to have additional, knock on effects on productivity. What is perhaps more interesting and certainly more controversial is the lack of obvious complementarity between these investments and investments in plant and machinery. While we do not want to seriously dispute the view that technology must often be embodied in capital equipment to affect productivity, it has to be said that our data do not provide much support for it—few of the firms who brought forward investments in innovation also brought forward investments in plant. This may be an artefact of the qualitative measures of investment activity that we have been using, or it may be taken to suggest that different types of innovations are introduced at different times of the cycle (capital using innovations being more frequently implemented in booms rather than slumps). More likely, in our view, is the possibility that the new product innovations in our data are modest advances to product ranges which require only modest adaptations of existing equipment. This means that they are likely to be accompanied by new processes and training but not new plant and equipment and, since they represent only modest advances to existing product ranges, they do not require heavy advertising or marketing. None of this should be taken to imply that recessions induce firms to implement only rather modest inventions, but it should cool the enthusiasm of those who talk about recessions and 'gales of creative destruction' in the same breath.

7 Conclusions

Summary

Economists have always had a lively interest in understanding the causes and consequences of trade cycles, and this has been particularly true in the last decade or two. Although many macroeconomists have tried to trace the origins of cyclical variations in aggregate economic activity to their microeconomic sources, their models are often extremely stylised and somewhat implausible. In particular, it is hard to believe that the simple representative firm models that macroeconomists use to analyse investment, employment or output determination go very far in identifying the microeconomic roots of movements in the associated macroeconomic aggregates. None of these models casts any useful light on the extraordinary heterogeneity of the effects of recessionary pressures on firms, and none seem to allow for the richness in response which one observes. This is a serious drawback, since recessions seem to be periods of disorganised (but not necessarily unsystematic) change.

Our goal in this volume has been to take a resolutely microeconomic look at what happens to firms during recessions, identifying which firms are most severely affected and observing how they respond to extreme adversity. Most of our observations have been drawn from the 600 or so replies that we received to a large-scale questionnaire sent out to more than 2,000 of the largest UK firms in the Spring of 1993. The survey was designed to yield qualitative and often somewhat subjective answers to questions which could be analysed in parallel with more conventional data about firms taken from balance sheets. Further, the survey tried to gather information on at least some of the characteristics of firms that are rarely available, and we used these to help identify vulnerable firms and help to explain why particular firms choose to make particular types of responses to the pressures that they faced.

143

In Chapter 1, we organised the work we planned to do around four issues, and this also seems to be a sensible way to organise the summary of
our main results.

Selection

Many people regard the competitive process as a selection mechanism in
which the disciplines of market competition weed out less efficient firms
and create room for more able firms to grow and develop new strengths.
For this kind of process to occur, the performance of firms using different
processes and offering different products in the same market must differ
(else there will be no grist for the selection mill to grind on). Indeed, the
more effective markets are at discriminating between the performance of
firms who do different things, the more effective market selection mechanisms will be at choosing which of those different things is best.

In fact, it is a very clear and robust feature of our data that performance
differences between firms increase markedly in recessions. While mean
profitability is procyclical, the variance in profitability across firms at any
time rises sharply in cyclical downturns. Indeed, that variance seems to have
risen secularly over the past decade or so, spurred on by two substantial
increases which occurred during the recessions of 1981 and 1991. One also
sees much the same phenomena in the observation that only relatively few
firms are very badly affected by recessionary pressures. Only one in five of
the firms who responded to our survey reported that they were 'extremely
severely' affected by the 1991 recession, and most of the sales, profit and
job losses were concentrated among the 10 per cent of worst performing
firms.

For selection to be effective, performance differences must be large
enough to discriminate between firms; for selection to be efficient, performance differences must correspond closely to differences in the activities
undertaken by different firms. If performance differences reflect the fundamentals, then selection will improve overall market performance; if,
however, transitory or idiosyncratic factors dominate performance differences, then selection may have a less beneficial effect. What is worse, if
performance differences reflect factors which mainly affect short-run cash
flows and do not accurately reflect long-run potential performance, then
selection processes may be overly myopic or shortsighted.

The evidence which we have managed to generate on this question is not
entirely clearcut. It is very difficult to talk cogently about the efficiency of
market selection because it is very difficult to measure efficiency at the level

of the firm in a satisfactory way. We have made more progress on the more modest question of identifying which firms tend to be most vulnerable to recessionary pressures, although here again we have not been as successful as we would have liked. There seems to be a weak tendency for firms who performed poorly just prior to the 1991 recession to perform poorly in the recession, although this is not a strongly noticeable feature of the data, and there are no scars evident from the 1981 recession which might enable one to identify struggling firms in 1991. However, recessions seem to scramble corporate performance rankings in complicated ways, and many apparently strong performers prior to the recession were also badly affected. Needless to say, this makes predicting which firms are going to be vulnerable rather difficult.

One fairly clear feature of the data is that selection works in two ways in recessions: more firms are put at risk, and the probability that an at-risk firm fails is higher in recessions than in booms. A second interesting feature of the data is that larger firms seem to be somewhat less vulnerable to recessionary pressures than smaller firms (although our data are drawn from a sampling frame of large firms and are not, therefore, terribly informative on this issue). Holding companies and companies with '*highly dispersed*' shareholdings seem slightly more vulnerable than others (foreign-owned subsidiaries are clearly less vulnerable), and some industries have been harder hit than others. It also seems clear that companies that grew fast prior to the recession, particularly those who were very acquisition active and took on a lot of debt, are more vulnerable to recessionary pressures than slower, more organic growers. Moreover, these conclusions seem to be the same whether one measures vulnerability by subjective assessment, falling profits or by the probability of failure.

All of this adds up to a vague sense that market selection procedures may be somewhat short-sighted. Companies which grow fast often make poor decisions (particularly those which grow mainly through acquisition) but it is, in general, hard to believe that they are failing in any real sense. It is certainly the case that fast growth can generate relatively high costs of adjustment, and our data suggests that firms who are unfortunate enough to time their growth spurts close to recessions may suffer for it. Markets do not seem to distinguish temporary declines in performance associated with adjustment costs from more serious and more fundamental deteriorations in performance. There is also a clear suggestion in the data that a lot of apparently random selection occurs, meaning that a surprisingly large number of firms who were apparently performing well prior to the recession suffered (what seem to us to be) large and mainly inexplicable declines in performance.

The response to adversity

Simple textbook discussions of the theory of the firm suggest that firms will respond to sharp falls in demand by reducing prices and quantities in a proportion which depends on the elasticity of supply. More sophisticated discussions of these issues usually argue that costs of adjustment can have two substantive effects on how firms adjust to shocks. First, the fact that adjustment is costly will make firms wish to distinguish transitory from permanent shocks, and avoid responding to the former. Second, costs of adjustment will condition how firms respond to shocks. Fixed costs of changing prices create incentives for firms to avoid responding to small shocks but, rather, to make large changes at very discrete intervals. On the other hand, costs which rise more than proportionately with the size of planned output or price changes create incentives for firms to smooth out the response to big shocks over time.

Our results are not consistent with either of these stories. The simple fact is that although many firms respond to recessionary pressures by reducing output and employment, most focus their energies on trying to reduce costs and do not adjust their prices much. For most firms (particularly those who are *'extremely severely'* affected by the recession), this means closing establishments, reducing employment and trying to control wages growth, something that many of these firms seem to think of as a *'focus'* strategy. Most firms do not undertake much financial reengineering in recessions (except those who cease trading), and almost all of them are reluctant to cut dividends. Most firms also do not change their product market strategies and, in particular, there seems to be very little in the way of product line rationalisation undertaken, even by *'extremely severely'* affected firms.

It is not actually clear why firms should focus their efforts on controlling costs in recessions. One would have thought that the incentive to cut costs would be high at all times, and it is slightly puzzling that many firms seem to regard focusing on costs to be the right response to demand shocks. There are several possible explanations for this apparent puzzle. In part, the cost responses we observed are volume related, and, therefore, the focus on costs is a natural consequence of the quantity adjustments which firms must make to declines in demand. Further, recessions have effects which look similar to those created by a major competitive shock (shifting residual demand in a manner analogous to that caused by large-scale entry), and this may strengthen incentives to reduce x-inefficiency and eliminate slack. That is, it may be that competitive pressures in most markets are sufficiently weak during cyclical upturns to diminish the incentives that managers have to control costs. If this is truly the case, it is not surprising to find that recession induced increases in competition have strong effects on managerial behaviour. Finally, it is clear that firms who were '*extremely severely*' affected by the recession were most active in cutting costs, and it is also the case that such firms sometimes grew relatively fast prior to the recession, had highly dispersed ownership structures and were (loosely) organised as holding companies. There is a sense, then, that many of them may have grown too big too fast, and were in need of rationalisation.

As is well known, investment in plant and equipment usually falls off rather markedly in recessions, and this seems to be true for our sample of firms. However, it is a clear feature of our data that investment in intangibles like training, advertising and marketing and R&D is much less severely affected by recessionary pressures than investment in plant or in buildings. Although it is almost certainly the case that the total volume of investment (tangible plus intangible) falls in recessions, the ratio of tangible to intangible investment seems to vary procyclically over time. What is more, a substantial minority of firms actually brought forward investments in product and process innovation in the recession. On the whole these innovative firms seem not to have been badly affected by the recession, and many of them thought that the recession was over.

We also observed quite a lot of structural change within firms. Slightly more than two thirds of them changed their organisational structure over the period 1985–93, although twice as many firms reorganised during the late 1980s (takeover) boom as during the subsequent recession. Smaller, functionally organised firms with a relatively tightly held share ownership structure seem to be organisationally more stable than other firms, and they were less likely to close or sell establishments. Management buyouts and contracting out do not appear to be common responses to recessionary pressures and, indeed, it seems likely that management buyouts vary procyclically over time. Finally, changes in production processes are also not particularly sensitive to recessionary pressures, although changes in labour organisation are.

At best, all of this seems to add up to weak support for the 'pit-stop' theory of recessions, and the associated predilection to think of recessions as periods of major structural change. Most discussions of the opportunity costs of making changes in recessions concentrate on labour adjustment: on retraining, on rematching workers to tasks and so on. This insight seems to have some foundation in the data, although most labour adjustment is just job shedding. However, extending these arguments to predict that major organisational changes or major restructuring of product lines and production processes is likely to be concentrated in recessions attracts little support from the data. Many of these changes are, in fact, induced by merger and acquisition (at least in the UK), and are, therefore, more likely to be pro-cyclical than countercyclical.

Feedback to the labour market

Possibly the most visible manifestation of recessions is the increase in un-employment which accompanies them. Economists have long debated the reasons why this occurs and, in particular, why changes in wages do not clear labour markets (or at least ameliorate the decline in employment). This is also a puzzle which emerges from our data. In common with others, we have found job shedding to be highly concentrated, with a relatively few firms accounting for a disproportionately large share of job losses. What is more, we have observed that these same firms took actions to control wages growth; that is, price and quantity adjustment seem to have been complementary responses to recessionary pressures rather than substitutes. Part of the resolution of this puzzle must lie in the uneven incidence of recessionary pressures, since the firms who laid off large numbers of work-ers and tried to control wages growth were *extremely severely* affected by the recession. Part of the answer also seems to lie in the behaviour of unions, since unionised firms instituted fewer wage freezes and shed fewer jobs. All of this said, however, the fact remains that the control over wages which firms managed was fairly modest, and it is unlikely to have had much impact on reducing wage costs.

The other interesting feature of our data on job shedding is that it does not seem to be consistent with the usual cost of adjustment stories, most of which predict that firms will smooth out their response to shocks, ad-justing their stock of employees frequently but by small amounts. In fact, the data paint a clear picture of a small number of firms who make infre-quent but large-scale changes in employment, usually by closing (or selling off) plants. This almost certainly implies that adjustment costs are, in the main, relatively fixed, but it may also be a consequence of highly integrated production processes which put large penalties on sub-optimal utilisation or limit the scope for marginal downsizing.

Given the large impact that recessions have on labour markets, it would be surprising to discover that the relative bargaining power of labour and management did not vary over the cycle. As one might have expected, our data suggest that union recognition fell slightly in the recession, largely as a consequence of plant disposal. Union membership also fell, mainly in those firms which partially derecognised unions. However, exiting firms and firms that completely derecognised unions made relatively little impact on either union recognition or membership overall. It is also the case that the location of wage setting agreements changed somewhat during the recession and, in particular, there was a rise in the incidence of firm and especially plant level wage setting (and a corresponding fall in the incidence of national agreements). Establishing exactly how much of this was due to the recession is not easy, since union recognition, union membership and the use of national wage agreements have all been declining for more than a decade. However, it seems to be the case that most of the changes in labour market institutions are secular and not cyclical, although the recession did hasten some of them.

Innovation

Many people believe that adversity brings the best out in individuals, and, therefore, that competition provides exactly the right kinds of incentives for firms to excel. Although textbook descriptions of the outcome of the competitive process focus on the equalisation of prices with marginal costs, less formal discussions often suggest that competition stimulates firms to be innovative. Recessions mimic many of the features of a sharp, sudden increase in competition, and they are, therefore, an interesting 'natural experiment' to use in probing the association between competitive adversity and innovation. Our data suggest that innovative activity is procyclical, and follows increases in demand. The firms in our sample which brought forward investments in product and process innovations were not, as a rule, very severely affected by the recession and most of them thought that it was over. Their response to recessionary pressures seems to be less an act of creative desperation designed to get them out of a competitive black hole, and more an opportunistic response to the difficulties of their rivals. To the extent that recessions breed innovative activity, it seems that they do so largely because of the uneven incidence of the effects of the recession on different firms. Given this, it is of no little interest to try to identify what type of firm is likely to bring forward innovative activity in the recession. This, however, turns out to be very difficult to do. There are almost no systematic associations between the likelihood that a firm brings forward investments in new products and processes and its observable characteristics, save that between innovativeness and how severely affected the firm was by recessionary pressures.

Investments in new product and new process innovations are rarely undertaken in isolation from other types of investment. Indeed, it is not entirely fanciful to suggest that investments in innovation may trigger off other forms of investment which, in turn, help to stimulate the economy and bring forward the end of the recession. Our data suggest that investments in new products and processes are often accompanied by investments in training and, less clearly, by investments in R&D and (even less clearly) marketing. There is no clear sign that these innovations are embodied in new plant and equipment. In fact, they seem more likely to be embodied in new skills than in new machines.

These observations cast some light on Schumpeterian hypothesis that recessions unleash 'gales of creative destruction'. Although the data are hardly decisive, the fact that innovative activity is roughly procyclical seems inconsistent with the view that recessions are a seedbed of innovative activity. Further, there are no grounds for believing that innovative activity drives increases in demand. Finally, we have observed enough internal, strategy driven change in our data to feel fairly confident in asserting that Schumpeterian stories which focus on new entrants bringing innovations to market and displacing older firms miss a great deal of the innovative activity which occurs during recessions.

Do firms emerge from recessions leaner and fitter?

One of the clearest and more surprising features of our data on the performance of UK firms is the steadily widening performance differentials which have been evident for more than a decade. Although the relative ranking of firms does not vary much over time (it varies much more during recessions than during booms), the spread of differences between firms widened during the Thatcher recession of 1981 and again during the Major-Lamont recession of 1991 without ever returning to pre-1980 levels. Amongst other things, this might mean that some firms emerged from recessions almost permanently stronger than they were prior to the recession, whilst others were possibly permanently enfeebled. It is worth closing with a few very speculative remarks on what might underlie this phenomena.

One often hears the expression that those firms who emerge from recession are leaner and fitter, the (unexpressed) presumption being that they are the better for having undergone the experience. It is rather hard to know what this means in practice. Most people who think this way go on to attribute this happy outcome to the fact that recessions force firms to cut into fat but, presumably, not into muscle. The problem with this view is that it is not exactly clear what fat and muscle are in the context of a company's operations. Nevertheless, it is important to ask whether what happens to a company during recessions has an effect, good or bad, on its long-run performance. Unfortunately, our data have relatively little to say about these issues, since we cannot link what happened to firms during the recession with their post-recession performance (not least because our survey took place as the recession was only just ending).

The data do, however, provide some support for two observations that are worth making. First, there is no question that firms are leaner when they emerge from recessions. Many of the firms in our sample shed jobs, and a few made large-scale redundancies. It is not, however, clear whether becoming leaner in this sense means becoming fitter. The job shedding which occurs in recessions is undoubtedly a major cause of the procyclical variations in productivity which has been widely observed. Job shedding may be no more than a reduction of labour which has been hoarded, and it may stimulate workers who remain in the firm to work harder. However, cyclical spurts of productivity growth are almost always transitory, and this means that the increased competitiveness created by recession induced labour shedding is likely to be inherently short lived.

Second, we have been able to trace the performance of many of our firms back through the Thatcher recession of 1981. If surviving that experience had had a major beneficial effect on how firms operate by forcing them to shed unproductive fat, one might have expected to find some traces of enhanced performance in the early 1990s. Conversely, if the pressures of that exceptionally severe recession had forced firms to cut into muscle and sacrifice long-term competitive ability for short-term survival, one might have expected firms that were badly affected by the 1981 recession to be particularly susceptible to the downturn in 1991. We observed neither effect. Immediate prerecession performance turns out to be, at best, a rather noisy predictor of distress during a recession, and we were unable to uncover any substantive traces of effect running over the entire decade between the two recessions. Save for those firms who fail, it seems hard to see any permanent effects of recessions.

Thus, insofar as our data have something useful to say about the likely post-recession performance of firms, it is that they often become leaner but only temporarily fitter. That the effects of recessions might be transitory (and we do not have enough useful information to be at all sure about this) might be a consequence of two quite different things. First, since the effects of recession are highly selective and only a relatively few firms are *extremely severely* affected by the recession, the sample of firms that bear scars is, in fact, likely to be rather small. Second, the scars created by recessions may be hard to detect because recessions are no more or less likely to induce major structural and strategic changes in the operations of firms than are booms. The plausibility of this second view is much enhanced by the fact that mergers and acquisitions are major drivers of change of both corporate structures and strategies, and they tend to be procyclical in incidence.

It is worth recalling just how selective recessions are: only about 50 per cent of the firms in our sample were at least 'severely' affected by the recession, only 20 per cent were 'extremely severely' affected, only 10 per cent were responsible for most of the lost jobs and only 5 per cent failed. What is more, the number of large-scale job shedders in the 1991 recession was only a little higher than in the preceding boom. We conjecture that mild growth pauses are likely to be intermediate between booms and recessions in this respect. The point is that it is a quantitative and not a qualitative difference which we have observed between recessions and booms. Those who think that recessions are like diets or fitness regimes are mistaken if they believe that recessions are unusual in these respects.

All of this leads to one final observation. The intensification of competitive pressures which recessions undoubtedly induce are only one way to force firms to take the kinds of actions which make them leaner and fitter. Mergers and acquisitions which bring capital market pressures to bear on senior managers are another way to accomplish much the same end, while increases in product market competition are a third. Most people believe that product market competition is generally an effective stimulant of beneficial change, and the evidence suggests that mergers and acquisitions are not always particularly efficient or effective in creating new, highly competitive organisations. They are also often extremely expensive (merchant bankers, lawyers and the shareholders of takeover victims can sometimes be the main beneficiaries). What is more, integrating and restructuring the newly merged operations of two or more formerly independent firms is a lot harder in practice than it looks in business-school textbooks. Our general impression of the data examined in this book is that it is even less clear that recessions are a good way of turning lumbering corporate dinosaurs into sleek and trim competitors. Recessions hit a small number of firms very badly and, for the most part, these and other firms shed jobs and close plants when economic activity falls. Some organisational changes and changes in systems or processes occur during slumps, but most are not induced by the recession. Moreover those firms who face the most extreme pressures are generally not the ones who initiate new product or process innovations.

In short, it is hard to believe that recessions are a good substitute for vigorous competitive pressures in product markets, or that the extreme adversity they create for some firms (and many workers) is a good way to stimulate economic growth and development. Recessions are useful for social scientists interested in finding 'natural experiments' which help them analyse what happens to firms in crisis, but they are probably not good for much else.

Appendix: the survey

Coping with the recession: a survey into the effects of the current
recession on UK company behaviour

Introduction

The recession which started in 1990 has been the longest of the postwar
period. It is essential that we learn some lessons from this period to help
companies facing similar situations in the future. We need to gain insight
into this period from companies themselves, rather than contenting our-
selves with a broad macroeconomic view of the problems of the country
as a whole. The National Institute of Economic and Social Research and
the London Business School have combined to launch this major new research initiative concerning company strategies for survival and growth.
We would value your cooperation.

   This programme will study companies' strategies in a number of different ways, but central to the initiative is this survey, which will give
contemporaneous insights into the problems faced by companies, and identify the actions which they have taken to ease those problems in the midst
of an economic downturn. We would be most grateful if you could complete the questionnaire on behalf of your company. The responses to the
survey will be the basis of academic research. Under no circumstances will
the information provided be sold for profit. Furthermore, all responses will
be treated with the utmost confidentiality. No company will be named or
information given that could lead to the identification of a company.

   NIESR and the LBS are non-profit making institutions engaged in academic research. Both have been at the forefront of studies into company
behaviour and growth processes. The particular researchers on this project

will be Paul Gregg, a senior research officer at NIESR, and Professor Paul Geroski of the Centre for Business Strategies at the LBS.

The survey is divided into three main sections, each with ten to fifteen questions. These sections cover the problems caused by the recession and responses to it, issues of human resource management and of company organisation. If you are unable to answer all questions please give as much information as you can. It will all be of use. If your company has prospered in the last few years your answers will be valuable as a contrast with those less fortunate. A free copy of a report into the main findings of the survey will be sent out to responding companies toward the end of next year.

We look forward to receiving your response and would like to thank you in anticipation of your cooperation.

SECTION I

EFFECTS OF THE RECESSION

This section is designed to gain an insight into how your company has been affected by the on-going recession, what particular problems your company has faced, and what responses your company made to alleviate these problems. Questions about the actions and success of your competitors will also be asked here.

Origins and Responses to the Recession in your Company

1.   How severely have your company's operations been affected by the recession? (Please answer against a benchmark of normal trading conditions.)

Extremely severely	
Severely	
Moderately	
Not at all	

2.   When do you expect the recession to be over for your company?

Already over	
Within 6 months	
6 months to a year	
More than a year	

3.   How has the recession affected the following aspects of your company's trading position in the years 1990–92?

	Seriously	Somewhat	Not at all
Decline in UK sales			
Decline in o/seas sales			
Excess capacity			
Excess inventories			
Excess indebtedness			
Cashflow constraints			
Other aspects that caused concern not specified in 3? Please specify.			

4.   More specifically, which of the following factors have been a source of your
        company's current problems (tick as many options as is appropriate).

		Very important	Some importance	Not important
(a)	**Macroeconomic conditions**			
	High interest rates			
	High exchange rate			
	Low consumer confidence			
	Worldwide recession			
	International competition			
	Falling land/building prices			
(b)	**Decisions within the firm**			
	Over expansion of company through merger or acquisitions before 1990			
	Over expansion of range of products or services provided before 1990			
	Over investments in plant/ buildings before 1990			
	Insufficient product or process innovation			
	Poor control of costs			
(c)	**Actions of other firms**			
	Increased competition in your product market			
	Innovations introduced by rivals			
	Non or late payment by customers (ie bad debts)			
	Credit limits by banks etc.			
(d)	Please specify below any other factors that you feel have been important which are omitted from the list above.			

5.   Which of the following actions were taken in response to the problems your company has faced in the recession, and how important have they been in overcoming these problems?

	Action taken		Action not taken
	and very important	and of some importance	
(a) Financial decisions			
Disposal of assets			
Reduce dividend cover			
Introduce a rights issue			
Reschedule debt			
Increase short term borrowing			
(b) Strategic decisions			
Focus on core businesses			
Increase prices			
Change marketing strategies			
Merge with/acquire another company			
Rationalise product lines			
Develop overseas markets			
(c) Cost Control			
Close establishments			
Reduce employment			
Reduce employee wage growth			
Reduce inventories			
Scrap outdated machinery			
Reduce headquarters costs			
Contract out auxiliary services			
(d) Others (please specify)			

6. Please indicate if your company abandoned, postponed or brought forward any of the following types of investment plans in the period 1990–92.

		Abandoned	Postponed	Brought forward
a)	Investment in plant/machinery			
b)	Investment in buildings			
c)	Investment in R&D			
d)	New product innovation			
e)	New process innovation			
f)	Training staff members			
g)	Advertising/marketing expenditure			

7. Did your company engage in a major overhaul of any of the following aspects of internal work organisation in some or all your establishments in the period 1990–92?

		Yes in response to the recession	Yes but not as a response to the recession	No
a)	Management methods			
b)	Production processes			
c)	Labour organisation/ manning levels/ restrictive practices			
d)	Wage payment systems			

Please give brief details of any "yes" response made above.

PRODUCT MARKET ISSUES

8.   In the period 1990–92 did your company

	Yes	No
Introduce new product lines or services within *existing* product markets?		
Introduce new product lines or services into product markets *new* to your company?		
Leave the range of products or services supplied unchanged?		
Withdraw product lines or services but continued in *all* product markets?		
Withdraw from supplying product lines or services from *some* product markets?		

9.   (a) What proportion of your company's sales are exports from UK establishments to overseas (i.e. non-UK) markets?

                   ☐ per cent

(b) What proportion of your companies sales are produced in non-UK establishments?

                   ☐ per cent

(c) Please tick <u>any</u> of the following broad geographical market areas if they constitute 5% or more of company's sales.

        EEC   N.America   Rest of the world
        ☐   ☐   ☐

10.   On balance did your company face increased or decreased competition in its major product market(s) in the years 1990-92?

	Increased	Decreased	No change
a) From UK competitors			
b) From foreign competitors			

11.   Please indicate whether the following indicators of competition in your prin
cipal product market increased or decreased in the period 1990–92

	Increase	Decreased	No Change
Number of competitors			
List prices of competitors			
Advertising by competitors			
Product lines marketed by competitors			
Research and development by competitors			
Level of production by surviving competitors			

12.   Is your company planning further responses to the recession which have not
yet begun being implemented?

                  Yes   ☐   No   ☐

If 'yes' above please give brief details of planned actions that will affect;

i)	The financial management of the company (i.e. debt rescheduling, disposal of assets, rights issue etc).
ii)	Strategic plans for the company (i.e. pricing policy, mergers/ acquisitions, re-focusing/re-organisation of business sectors etc).
iii)	Cost control within the company (i.e. establishment closure, employment reductions, wages growth, reduction of inventories etc)

13.   On balance do you think that your company will emerge from the recession stronger and better placed to exploit new opportunities than before, or significantly weaker and less able to exploit new opportunities for some years to come?

Stronger   Unchanged   Weaker

☐ ☐ ☐

Why do you draw this conclusion? Please give details in the spaces below for the appropriate areas of your company's operation.

(i) Cost control within the company

(ii) Investment and R&D (including training and quality of staff)

(iii) Product market including competition from U.K. and overseas rivals, market ing and product range

(iv) Other factors not specified which you feel are important

SECTION II

ISSUES OF HUMAN RESOURCE MANAGEMENT

We would now like to ask some background questions about your workforce composition and pay setting arrangements.

The Workforce

1.   What percentages of your company's total workforce are: -

a) Managerial or professional employees	
b) Administrative and support (i.e. administrative, secretarial, supervisory or clerical)	
c) Skilled manual employees (i.e. requiring formal certificates or qualifications recognised by many employers)	
d) Unskilled manuals and counter staff	
e) Female	
f) Part-time employees (i.e. less than 30 hrs a wk)	
g) Members of trades unions	

2.   Did the proportion of your company's workforce which belonged to the following broad categories increase, decrease or remain the same in the period between 1990–92?

	Increase	Decrease	No change
a) Managerial or professional			
b) Administrative and support			
c) Skilled manual			
d) Unskilled manuals or counter staff			
e) Female			
f) Part-time			
g) Members of trades unions			

3.   Did your company use any of the following methods of workforce alteration in any establishment that continued in operation in the period 1990–92?

	Yes	No	Most widely used
Redeployment between job functions			
Recruitment freeze/natural wastage			
Early retirement			
Voluntary redundancy			
Compulsory redundancy			
Other (please specify)			

4.   Please indicate in the space below what criteria were used in selecting which employees were to be made redundant or offered incentives to leave?

5.   What percentage of your employees

a) left employment with the company in the last year?

b) started employment with the company in the last year?

6.   Does your company:

	Yes	No
Recognise trade unions for the purposes of bargaining over wages in any of your establishments?		
Operate an agreement with a union that some or all members of the workforce are expected to join a union?		

7.   In the period 1990–92 did your company:

	Yes	No
Cease to recognise any trade union for the purposes of bargaining over wages in any of your establishments (disregard where this is due to establishment closure or union merger)?		
Repudiate a union-management agreement that any members of the workforce were expected to join a trade union in any of the company's establishments?		

8.   Companies with recognised Trade Unions:
        Please indicate the *most* important level at which negotiations over wage increases for your workforce take place.

National/industry wide with more than one employer (including wages councils)	
This employer/division but more than one establishment	
Individual establishment but more than one group of employees	
Individuals or separate groups of employees	

        Companies with NO recognised Trade Unions:
        Please indicate the breadth of coverage of decisions determining wage increases for your workforce. (ie. do the applicable increases vary between individuals with the same characteristics, between establishments or do they also cover workers outside your firm).

National/industry wide with more than one employer (including wages councils)	
This employer/division but more than one establishment	
Individual establishment but more than one group of employees	
Individuals or separate groups of employees	

9.   Companies with recognised Trade Unions:
       Please indicate whether over the years 1990–1992 there was any change in
       the importance of the level at which negotiations over wages took place.

Level of wage setting	Increased importance	No change	Decreased importance
National/industry wide with more than one employer			
This employer but more than one establishment			
Individual establishment but more than one group of employees			
Individuals or separate groups of employees			

Companies with NO recognised Trade Unions:
Please indicate whether there has been any change in the breadth of coverage
of decisions determining wage increases across members of your workforce.

Level of wage setting	Increased importance	No change	Decreased importance
National/industry wide with more than one employer			
This employer but more than one establishment			
Individual establishment but more than one group of employees			
Individuals or separate groups of employees			

10.   (a) In the period 1990–2 did your company operate, at any time, a temporary 'wage freeze' covering a substantial part of the workforce?

       Please answer "Yes" if you are currently operating or about to introduce a
       'wage freeze'.

       [ ] Yes   [ ] No

(b) If yes, how long did the wage freeze last? If uncompleted or about to be
introduced, please indicate the anticipated duration.

3 months or less	
4–6 months	
7–12 months	
more than 12 months	

SECTION III

COMPANY ORGANISATION

This last section asks some background questions about the structure and organisation of your company. This information is necessary so that we can explore some of the reasons for variation in the success of companies in dealing with the recession.

1.   Which of the following options best describes the ownership of the company?

a) UK subsidiary of an overseas company	
b) UK owned with a majority holding by current company directors	
c) UK owned with a significant minority holding by current company directors	
d) UK owned with one individual (other than a director) or institution holding a majority or a significant minority stake	
e) UK owned with highly dispersed ownership among individuals or institutional investors	

2.   Does your company operate an Employee Share Ownership Programme for any part of its workforce other than directors?

Yes   No

If 'yes' what percentage of your company's employees participate?

3.   (a) How many years has the current Chief Executive Officer (CEO) been in charge? (If the exact year is unknown please give an approximation)

(b) Was the CEO appointed from within this organisation or from outside?

Within   Outside

4.   Please indicate which of the following basic organisational structures most closely resembles that of your company within the UK:

a) A functional structure ☐

CEO

Sales   Finance   Marketing   Production

b) A holding company structure ☐

Holding company

Company 1   Company 2
Sales, finance, etc.   Sales, Finance, etc.

If ticked, how many companies ☐
c) A divisional structure ☐

Corporate head office

Division   Division   Division
Sales, finance, etc.   Sales, finance, etc.

If ticked, how many companies ☐
c) A divisional structure with groups and/or sectors ☐

Corporate head office

Group level   Group

Division   Division   Division
Sales finance,   Sales, finance,   Sales, finance,
   etc.   etc.   etc.

d) Other (please give details) ☐

5.   If your company's organisational structure has changed since 1985 what was the primary reason for the change?

a) Merger or takeover of another company	
b) Potential hostile takeover by another company	
c) New Chief Executive Officer	
d) Expansion of company	
e) Contraction of company	
f) Re-organisation induced by recession	
g) Other (please specify)	
h) Not changed	

6.   How many separate establishments does your company operate in the UK?

7.   Please indicate if your establishments are sited in the following regions of the UK (tick as many options as you like).

Dispersed across all regions	
South East (including London)	
South West or Wales	
Midlands (East and West) or East Anglia	
Northern England (North West, Yorks and Humber or the North)	
Scotland or N. Ireland	

8   In the period 1990–2 did your company engage in any of the following actions concerning the size of its operations:

	Yes	No
Sell any part of its operation to another company(ies)?		
Have a management buyout of any part of its operation?		
Contract out to another company functions or services previously undertaken within company?		
Close one or more establishments?		

9.   What was the *net change* in the number of establishments your company operated in the period 1990–2.

We would like to thank you again for your co-operation. If you would like a free copy of a report summarising the results of the survey please tick the box below.

Notes

1 INTRODUCTION

1   For some reflections on the use of natural experiments, see Meyer, 1995.

2   For commentaries on this period, see Buiter and Miller, 1983, Feinstein and Matthews, 1990, Sargent, 1991, Blackburn and Ravin, 1992, Sentance, 1992, Currie and Sentance, 1994, and others; see also *Economic Outlook* and the *National Institute Economic Review* for regular commentaries on the state of the UK economy. Crafts, 1992, examines UK productivity growth performance over the period in a broader European context.

3   The data used in this section was drawn from the CSO databank at the Centre for Economic Forecasting at London Business School. We are obliged to John O'Sullivan for his help in extracting it.

4   For work on the link between inflation and relative price variation, see Fisher, 1981, and others; Domberger, 1987, reports work done on the UK.

5   Work on the costs of recessions often focuses on measuring the cost of the risks created for agents by cyclic fluctuations; see Lucas, 1987, Clark *et al*, 1994, and others. These numbers sometimes turn out to be extremely small, and it is hard to believe that such costs are more important than the loss of output caused by idle or underused physical or human capacity.

6   This view is gradually being assimilated into theories of economic growth which focus on the displacement of old by new technologies in uneven bursts of activity over time; see Aghion and Howitt, 1992, Segerstrom, 1990, and Segerstrom *et al*, 1991; Grossman and Helpman, 1991, provides an overview of some of this work. These models focus on the displacement of older innovations by newer ones; in a similar spirit, Aghion and Saint Paul, 1991 and 1993, argue that the reorganisation and implementation of new activities which lead to productivity improvements are more likely to occur during recessions than during expansions.

7   Penrose, 1959, is a classic account of the internal costs of adjustment which arise as firms expand. Although her argument is frequently cited in connection with the assertion that there are managerial limits to growth, it does carry the impli-

171

cation that firms will wish to postpone the reallocation of senior management time to periods when the opportunity cost is low: that is, that growth spurts will be smoothed and some of the necessary internal reorganisation accompanying growth may be postponed until recessionary (or low growth) periods.

8   See Hall, 1991a, and 1991b, who focuses on changes associated with the increased volume of job matching that occurs during recessions; see also Bean, 1990, Caballero and Hammour, 1994, Cooper and Haltiwanger, 1990, 1992, and 1993, and others.

9   Entry seems to matter most in very new markets, or in fragmenting and apparently technologically stagnant markets; see Geroski, 1991.

10   Selection induced by product market competition almost certainly has this feature: consumers generally reward firms who actually produce good products inexpensively, not those who merely promise to do so (however credible the promise). Matters are more complex in the case of capital market selection, since, in principle, the market value of a firm depends upon current expectations of future profits. There is, however, a large literature concerned with short-termism; that is, with whether stock market valuations are myopic. For a brief overview, see Nickell, 1995, Chapter 2.

11   Porter, 1980, identifies three types of generic strategy, including 'focus' along with the two identified in the text. The view that cost leadership and differentiation are mutually exclusive strategies springs from the belief that cost leadership is driven by learning or economies of scale whose effects on cost depend on product standardisation. Differentiation turns on customising products for particular groups of consumers, and, the literature on mass customisation not withstanding, almost certain involves some loss of scale economies. For some critical comments on this view, see Baden-Fuller and Stopford, 1992, and others.

12   This is particularly evident to those who have had first-hand experience with recent policy initiatives like deregulation and privatisation where workers (but not top managers) have often suffered wage and employment cuts when their firms were exposed to competition; see Bailey, 1986, Vickers and Yarrow, 1988, and others for some evidence.

13   Possibly the most obvious manifestation of these changes is the pro-cyclicality of strike activity which, presumably, reflects shifts in relative bargaining power; see Harrison and Stewart, 1989 and 1994, Dickerson, 1994 and others.

14   Recent surveys of this literature (theoretical and empirical) include Scherer, 1992, Beath et al, 1995, and Cohen, 1995.

15   Schmookler, 1966, has inspired a range of demand-pull arguments, while Rosenberg, 1974, has argued for the importance of supply-push factors; see also Mowery and Rosenberg, 1987, for a discussion of some of these issues in a rather broader context.

16   For work on 'long waves', see Solomou, 1987, Rosenberg and Frischtak, 1984, Kleinknecht et al, 1992, and the useful summary in Tylecote, 1991.

2   THE RECESSION SURVEY

1   Parts of the survey (notably the third section) were based on the questionnaire devised by Costas Markides, and applied to data on large US firms; see Markides, 1995.

2   Unsurprisingly, firms that went into receivership usually failed to provide complete company accounts prior to their demise. Often their last accounts were two or even three years out of date. This means that any study of their characteristics after 1990 (and certainly after 1991) is impossible. Equally, those firms that we could not find in 1993 also have no accounts after 1990. However, most firms who were taken over continued to provide separate company accounts through this period.

3   For a useful textbook discussions, see Milgrom and Roberts, 1992, Chapter 16, or Besanko *et al.*, 1996, Chapter 17, and references cited therein; Gould and Campbell, 1987, identify a number of different styles of managing diversified companies.

4   See Steer and Cable, 1978, Channon, 1973, and others for the UK. Recent work by Markides, 1995, on 136 large US firms found that just under 11 per cent of them were functionally organised, a figure which was up from 5per cent in 1970.

5   Of the 76 firms in our sample with sales in excess of £500m, 28 per cent were functionally organised, 18 per cent were holding companies and 48 per cent were divisionalised. By contrast, 40 per cent of the 75 companies with sales less than £10m were functionally organised and only 12 per cent were divisionalised.

6   32 per cent of the firms in our sample in retailing and services were functionally organised, while only 20 per cent had a divisionalised structure. By contrast, 31 per cent of the manufacturing firms in our sample were divisionalised and only 32 per cent were functionally organised. Within manufacturing there was little variation in the proportions of firms that were divisionally or functionally organised.

7   Thus, for example, Prais, 1976, found that only 11 of the largest UK firms in 1972 had Directors who had an ownership stake of 10 per cent or more, while Cubbin and Leech, 1983, found that only 10 of 85 large UK companies taken from the Times top 400 had a single shareholder who owned more than 20 per cent of shares. For a recent survey of the UK and US literature, see Hay and Morris, 1991.

8   Of the firms in our sample with less than £10m in sales, only 31 per cent reported a 'highly dispersed' ownership structure, while 59 per cent of the firms whose sales exceeded £500m were 'highly dispersed'. 'Highly dispersed' ownership structures were more common in manufacturing (42 per cent) than in non-manufacturing (32 per cent).

9   Similarly, Hay and Kamshad, 1994, surveyed 408 small and medium sized UK firm in three sectors (printing, software and instruments) in March 1993 and found that only 12 per cent of them were *'extremely severely'* affected by the recession (26 per cent were *'severely'* affected).

10 As noted in Chapter 1, this may be one of the more significant differences be-
    tween the 1980 and 1990 recessions. The appreciation in sterling which started
    in 1977 and continued through 1980 had a severe effect on export activity which
    seems not to have occurred in the early 1990s.

3   COMPANY PERFORMANCE OVER THE BUSINESS CYCLE

1   See Campbell and Mankiw, 1987, Cochrane, 1988, and others on the evolu-
    tion of aggregate output; Dunne and Hughes, 1994, Geroski *et al*, 1995 and
    Hart and Oulton, 1995, discuss recent work on the growth of firms in the UK.
2   An interesting illustration of this phenomena is discussed by Bresnahan and Raff,
    1991, who document how the restructuring in the US car industry occasioned
    by the Great Depression cleared the way for the emergence of mass production
    techniques. Most of the plant closures which occurred were concentrated
    amongst smaller, less efficient craft-production plants, whose exit made way for
    the entry and expansion of plants embodying mass production techniques. See
    also the discussion of the US Steel industry in Davis *et al*, 1996, Chapter 5.
3   Caballero and Hammour, 1994, examine the extent to which cyclical variations
    in new firm creation rates insulate older, less efficient firms from the process of
    destruction, an issue which turns on the structure of adjustment costs in their
    model. In particular, if adjustment costs are high, entry decisions become less
    sensitive to current economic conditions, and, as a consequence, fall off by less
    when the economy turns down. Data on job creation and destruction suggests
    that the latter is much more cyclically responsive than the former, meaning that
    the insulating effect of job creation may be rather weak (see also Davis and
    Haltiwanger, 1992).
4   For recent discussions of these issues, see Nickell, 1995, and Kay, 1993, Chap-
    ter 2.
5   Many of these problems turn on the treatment of capital depreciation, and the
    distortions which can arise from the use of different rules; see Fisher and
    McGowan, 1983, Fisher, 1987, Edwards *et al*, 1987, and others. Variations in
    capital intensity across firms will, of course, generate permanent variations in
    profit margins between firms. It is also arguably the case that forward looking
    measures of corporate performance (like stockmarket rates of return) are supe-
    rior to the more static, backward looking measures of accounting profitability
    that are more frequently used in this context. Unfortunately, we cannot use these
    stock market based measures of performance, since nearly a third of the firms
    in our sample are not quoted.
6   See Penrose, 1959, for a classic discussion of these issues.
7   These are drawn from the EXSTAT database. EXSTAT contains annual com-
    pany accounts for around 4000 companies over this period, with about 2500
    firms present in any one year. However, EXSTAT progressively included smaller
    companies into its database over the period 1971–1981. To make consistent
    calculations, we have selected only firms with over 500 employees, and with at

least 4 continuous records over the period. This generates a sample of 2294.

8   The employment figures are for the period 1989 to 1992.

9   For example, work in the US by Davis and Haltiwanger, 1992, has shown that while job creation and job destruction occur simultaneously in every industry in every year (usually at rates greater than 6 per cent), job creation is much less variable over time than job destruction. Further, job destruction seems to be very highly concentrated: only 23 per cent of the jobs lost in recessions were lost in establishments which shrank by 20 per cent or less. More interestingly, only 25 per cent of gross job losses were caused by the death of an establishment, while the rest of the job losses occurred in dramatically shrinking establishments; see also Davis *et al.*, 1996. Similarly, Burgess and Blanchflower, 1993, found that about 50 per cent of all jobs destroyed in the UK over the period 1980–90 were accounted for by 10 per cent of plants.

10   See Mueller, 1986 and 1990, Geroski and Jacquemin, 1988, and others.

11   We also ran the usual persistence of profits autoregressions on our data, and found estimates of the autoregression parameter to be slightly lower in recessionary periods than in booms. For example, the coefficient on lagged profits (5 years ago) in 1981 was 0.714 (standard error = 0.030), and in 1991 it was 0.708 (0.054). In non-recession years, the coefficient varied from 0.79 in 1983 to 0.85 in 1988.

12   For a discussion of the technique of studying the persistence of profitability (or other measures of performance) by computing Markov transitions between points in the distribution over time, see Quah, 1993 and 1994.

13   This is more strikingly true when one focuses on the bottom decile. In 1976, 1986 and 1989, the percentage of the bottom decile of firms that were in the bottom quartile 5 years earlier was in the range of 65–70 per cent. In the recession years of 1981 and 1991, the percentage drops to about 35 per cent.

14   Comparing Tables 3.3 and 3.4, it is evident that while mobility from any quartile into the bottom quartile is higher in the long run than in the short, the differences are not large. For work using transition matrices to make inferences about the degree of mobility amongst top ranked firms within industries in the UK, see Geroski and Toker, 1994.

15   The slope of an OLS regression (including a constant) between the two sets of profit changes is 0.0414, with a standard error of 0.0238, which is insignificantly different from zero.

16   Needless to say, stock market rates of return are interesting in this context, since they reflect the current expectations about future profitability held by capital market operators. Whether these expectations are the same as those held by managers is an interesting question which we unfortunately cannot answer.

17   In principle, *vulnerability* might mean *susceptible to recessionary shocks*, or it might mean *unable to respond to shock and maintain pre-recession performance levels*. Although we asked questions about the causes of recessionary pressures before moving on to ask about responses in our survey, it is possible that we did not separate these questions clearly enough. As a consequence, and despite our intention to focus on the first meaning, it may be that our respond-

ents conflated these two meanings somewhat.

18   The correlation coefficient between the subjective measure of the severity of the
     recession and 1991 profit margins is 0.3141, while those between the subjec-
     tive measure and the change in margins, 1989–91, and real sales growth over
     the same period are 0.2546 and 0.3038. These correlations are based on 564
     observations with sales and profits data for 1989 and 1991.

19   Repeated experiments on a range of empirical models suggested that only the
     distinction between holding companies and the rest had any explanatory power.
     Similarly, only the distinction between domestic and foreign owned firms re-
     ally mattered.

20   The relationship between firm size and vulnerability to the recession has been
     fairly widely (if sometimes casually) documented; see Lane and Schary, 1993,
     and referees cited therein; Gertler and Gilchrist, 1994, studied the effects of tight
     monetary policy in the US, and found that the sales inventory holding and short
     term debt of smaller firms decline relative to those of larger firms.

21   This sample differs slightly from that discussed in Chapter 2. The latter used
     1989 (and not 1990) as the base year.

22   The survival rate (until 1991) of firms not in the bottom decile of the ranking
     by profit margins in 1987 was 88 per cent; 3 per cent went into receivership, 6
     per cent were taken over and 2 per cent were untraceable.

23   The differential on the coefficients being different on the loss making firms be-
     tween the two periods in a combined equation is 0.2488 (with a standard error
     = 0.1484).

24   Both high debt and smaller firms are over-represented among the loss making
     firms: just under 12 per cent of all firms had a debt-assets ratio above one stand-
     ard deviation above the mean, while among loss makers, it was just under 20
     per cent. Likewise 19 per cent were smaller than one deviation below the mean,
     whilst among loss makers it was 37 per cent. Size is, however, interesting, as
     the best performers also include more small firms: being small increases the like-
     lihood of being in either tail of the performance distribution in a recession, but
     being small and making loses is rather likely to prove fatal.

25   Even with industry dummies equations for severity of impact of the recession
     only reach pseudo R square of 7 per cent.

26   See Davis et al, 1996, especially Chapter 5, for a discussion and references.

27   When coupled with various market frictions (search costs, sunk investments in
     skills or information acquisition, and so on), these allocative shocks can gener-
     ate persistent unemployment. Similarly, investment lags and problems associated
     with the production of highly user specific capital can translate transitory shocks
     in to more persistent spells of low output growth.

4   CHANGES IN CORPORATE STRATEGY AND STRUCTURE

1   See Sutton, 1991, for a discussion of the effect of sunk costs on market struc-
     ture more generally.

2   In fact, the discussion in the text is a little too simple, since firms typically change their strategy over the cycle; for some results for the US oil-well drilling business over the 1972–83 period; see Mascarenhas and Aaker, 1989.

3   See Porter, 1980, who argues that focus (on market niches) is a third generic strategy.

4   See Biggadike, 1976, Yip, 1982, Cubbin and Domberger, 1988, Singh *et al.*, 1991 and Bunck and Smiley, 1992.

5   For example, Erickson, 1976, observed cost reductions of 10–25 per cent in three US industries where entry disrupted patterns of collusive pricing, and much the same effects have been observed in deregulated industries in the US and privatised industries in the UK (see Bailey, 1986, and Vickers and Yarrow, 1988).

6   The data for 1982 is a little problematic as the definition of the firms' employment changed at this time for a minority of firms and is not included. These firm employment numbers are also troublesome because firm expansion covers growth through acquisition of firms or purchases of other firm subsidiaries. A firm that disappears does not register in the employment growth averages, but does appear in the statistics for the acquiring firm. Thus, merger and acquisition will naturally produce a small number of firms with rapid employment growth. Although the same is true on the downside, a firm will only be in the data where part of a company is sold. Hence, average employment growth is biased upwards, especially in merger booms such as 1987–9.

7   For detailed work at establishment level which points a not dissimilar picture of job creation and destruction, see Davis *et al.*, 1992 and 1996, and Burgess and Blanchflower, 1993.

8   In much the same spirit, Bhaskor *et al.*, 1993, surveyed 73 small, owner-managed Scottish firms in 1985, and found that quantity adjustments were '*overwhelmingly more important*' than price adjustments to cyclical shocks, particularly in recessions. See also Geroski and Hall, 1985; for work on price dynamics in the UK, see Geroski, 1992 and, for US work on cyclical fluctuations in profit margins, see Domowitz *et al.*, 1986.

9   The argument that recessions are a time of capital cleansing and extensive machine replacement articulated by Caballero and Hammour, 1994, and Cooper and Haltiwanger, 1993, turns on a non-connexity in adjustment costs (see also Bertola and Caballero, 1990, and Caballero and Engel, 1993). This effectively means that agents will not respond continuously to shocks, but, rather, will make relatively less frequent, more large-scale changes than would occur in the absence of adjustment costs. The very high relative importance of plant closure to capital scrapping shown on Table 4.1 is (weakly) consistent with this view. It also seems to be consistent with work by Bresnahan and Ramey, 1994, on the weekly operations of 50 US automobile plants from 1972 –83. They observe that varying overtime hours is a less important form of adjustment than adding or dropping a shift, or shutting the plant down for a week.

10   When we compiled the questionnaire, we did not expect to observe many changes in company organisation induced by the recession. The extremely high incidence of restructuring reported by our respondents surprised us, and made us wish

that we had been more precise in dating the changes, gauging their size and monitoring the new structures that the three types of firm identified on Figure 4.1 chose.

11   Murphy and Zimmerman, 1993, examined the movements of a range of financial variables around the time of the CEO's departure for 1,063 executives in 599 US firms over the period 1965–89. They observed declines in the growth rate of R&D, advertising and capital expenditures preceding departure which seem to be related to the poor corporate performance. Further, they suggest that new CEOs often take a 'big bath', in the sense that accounting returns often fall immediately upon secession. All of this is consistent with the view of new CEOs as agents of change.

12   Only 47 per cent of 'extremely severely' affected firms had a CEO of five years duration or less (43 per cent of other firms had a CEO of less than 5 years duration).

13   See Markides, 1995, Bhagat et al., 1990, and the papers in Bishop and Kay, 1993, for views and evidence on the extent of the recent wave of corporate refocusing in the US, and on recent merger activity in the UK and Europe.

14   These results are broadly consistent with work reported by Nickell and Nicolitsas, 1995, and West et al., 1995, based on field studies of about 100 UK manufacturing organisations. They observed that decreasing market share often triggered management innovations like changing company structure, HRM practices and so on.

15   These results are slightly inconsistent with those reported by West et al., 1995, and Nickell and Nicolitsas, 1995, which suggest that product/product innovation is stimulated by poor current performance. However, neither our survey nor theirs is precise enough on the link between current performance, current expectations of future performance and current decisions to invent or implement new products or processes to be definitive on this issue.

16   Saint-Paul, 1993, has argued that countercyclical investment activities are liable to be those which are not cash-intensive and have a long horizon over which benefits are reaped (as Schliefer, 1986, has noted, if an investment has a short pay-off, the investor would like to time its introduction to the market to insure that the pay-off comes at the best time; that is during a boom). While the first argument seems plausible and is consistent with what we observe on Table 4.7, the second seems less obviously consistent with the data. It is hard to believe that R&D, marketing and training expenditures yield a longer pay-off than investment in plant.

17   This is consistent with the results obtained by Whittington, 1991, from a survey of 100 UK manufacturing firms in the winter of 1984. These firms indicated that introducing new products and improving existing products were their most important responses to the (1981) recession. Putting pressure on suppliers—likely to be a form of cost cutting—also ranked high on their lists.

18   These observations are similar to those made by Markides, 1995, who argues that many US firms over diversified in the 1960s and 1970s and, as a consequence, we were forced to focus on the 1980s.

5   THE LABOUR MARKET IN RECESSION

1   For a survey of some of these arguments (and their consequences for unemployment) see Blanchard and Fischer, 1989, Knight, 1987, Layard *et al.*, 1991, and others; Abraham and Haltiwanger, 1995, survey evidence on real wages over the cycle.

2   For recent work on these subjects, see Kelly, 1987, Millward *et al.*, 1993, Stewart, 1991, Machin and Wadhwani, 1991, Carruth and Disney, 1988, Metcalf, 1989, 1990, 1993, Disney *et al.*, 1993, Claydon, 1989, Gregg and Yates, 1991, Gallie *et al.*, 1996, and others.

3   Some of the material in these sections is drawn from Geroski *et al.*, 1995.

4   It is also worth noting that employment changes are not very persistent. Between 1986 and 1992, the one year correlation in annual employment growth across firms was just 0.18, with two years previous just 0.07 and at three years 0.02. In the 1970s, these correlations were even smaller. Hence, employment contractions in recessions are both highly concentrated, and not common to the same firms in each recession. In fact, the evolution of firms' employment is close to a random walk (as is the evolution of sales, assets and most other measures of firm size).

5   There has been an intense and inconclusive debate about the effects of unions on firm or plant growth in employment. Bronars and Deere, 1993, suggest no effect in the US, while Machin and Wadhwani, 1992, suggest union firms lost employment in the UK in the period 1980–84 because of a decline in their ability to influence employment through restrictive practices. On the other hand, Blanchflower and Oswald, 1992, argued that unions were directly responsible for slower employment growth in this period.

6   See Holt, 1970, Stewart, 1991 and 1992, and others.

7   This evidence strongly parallels US evidence from establishments. Davis and Haltiwanger, 1992 and 1996 show that job destruction is largely idiosyncratic to the establishment, rather than an industrial sector (see parallels with regressions in Table 1), and argue that the counter-cyclical nature of total labour reallocation (that is, total job destruction plus job creation) is produced by the interaction of the cycle and frictions in the labour market. The evidence presented in Chapter 3 suggests that such frictions are not necessary for this countercyclical relation. A recession period produces much wider variations in the idiosyncratic shocks felt by firms than upturns, re-ranking company performance and productivity to a surprisingly large degree. This produces greater polarisation of job losses and creation occurring at the same time.

8   This is not dissimilar to the picture painted by Caballero *et al.*, 1995 who examined US plant data on investment activities, and observed non-convexities and asymmetries in the adjustment of actual investment to 'mandated' investment at plant level; that is, for most of the time, firms did not acquire or divest equipment, but when they did act they did so on a large scale. This behaviour—like that cited in the text—is hard to reconcile with the usual quadratic costs of adjustment model.

9   Note that the entrant firms are not newly created firms; rather, they are just new to the EXSTAT database.

10   For an exposition of the technique that we have used, see Gomulka and Stern, 1991.

11   Earlier work has shown that derecognition became somewhat less infrequent after 1984, but that complete derecognition was still rare in the late 1980s; see Claydon, 1989, Gregg and Yates, 1991, and others.

12   Four firms were identified as giving inaccurate information in one or other of the surveys. Two of the four firms who gave inaccurate information were borderline cases where recognition existed but not for wages, one indicated a confusion between UK and worldwide operations and the last one definitely made a mistake in its responses.

13   Disney, Gosling and Machin, 1993, explored the decline in recognition among UK establishments up to 1990 using the WIRS surveys, and they argue that the attrition of union plants combined with a declining likelihood of new recognition was the main factor behind declining incidence of recognition. This difference in view may turn on the use of plant versus firm level data. As the decline in recognition in our surveys is largely confined to small firms, they will represent a larger proportion of the stock of firms than they will plants. Further, if the birth of new non-union plants is occurring in firms with unions recognised elsewhere within the firm, then this will not appear as more non-union firms (instead, firms would be observed as having a smaller proportion of unionised plants). This would be consistent with the view that unions are no longer securing spillover recognition from one part of an organisation to another, a phenomena which in turn may well be related to the fragmentation of bargaining that has occurred through the 1980s and early 1990s.

14   The figure cited in the text is somewhat larger than that derived from national sources. For example, using Labour Force Survey data, Bird et al., 1993, observed that union membership density fell from 38 per cent to 35 per cent between Spring 1990 and Autumn 1992. However, their numbers include public sector workers who claimed a growing share of total employment during the recession; in manufacturing, union density fell by 5 percentage points.

15   As the same weights are used for both dates, this fall in membership cannot be explained by relative employment shifts. Rather, it means that union density fell within firms, possibly due to differential job shedding across occupational groups within firms.

16   That the decline in membership is only a weakly correlated with changes in coverage tends to support the view of Disney, 1990, about the separation of these two components on union presence when assessing the decline in union membership; see also Mason and Bain, 1993, for a discussion of this debate.

17   The trend towards more decentralised pay setting in unionised firms has been in evidence since before the Donovan report, but it probably accelerated during the 1980s. Gregg and Yates, 1991, reported that more rapid decentralisation occurred between 1985 and 1989 than between 1980–84. Sisson and Brown, 1983, argue that decentralisation of bargaining allows a clearer link between

pay and performance to be established, and Gregg and Machin, 1992, found that pay decentralisation among union firms was undertaken by those who experienced high wage and low productivity growth prior to its introduction. These firms experienced considerably slower wage growth and more modest changes improvements in productivity after decentralisation.

6   INNOVATIVE ACTIVITY IN THE RECESSION

1   For recent surveys and evaluations of this literature see Cohen, 1995, Scherer, 1992, and others.

2   See, for example, Bernanke and Parkinson, 1991, Hall, 1986, Fay and Medoff, 1985, Burnside *et al.*, 1993, and references cited therein.

3   The evidence suggesting that these kinds of factors can enhance the productivity growth of firms is weak but not implausible; see Lichtenberg, 1992, on the effects of mergers, Lichtenberg, 1992b on divestment, Oulton, 1987, on plant closures, Nickell *et al.*, 1992, on debt competition and unionisation, Gregg *et al.*, 1993, on unions, closed shops and other labour market institutions, and others.

4   See Rosenberg, 1974, Dosi, 1988, and others.

5   This is, of course, a variant of the 'pit-stop' theory of recessions, and is not dissimilar to arguments made by Mensch, 1979, and others. See Clark *et al.*, 1981, and Freeman *et al.*, 1982, for critical evaluations of Mensch's work, and Kleinknecht, 1987, for a more sympathetic assessment.

6   See Arrow, 1963. Rent displacement is often used as an argument suggesting that incumbent firms will try to slow the pace of innovation. The counterargument which is sometimes made is that when new innovations complement (rather than substitute for) existing activities, incumbents may accelerate the pace of innovation, pre-empting their rivals. Tirole, 1988, refers to these as the 'replacement effect' and the 'efficiency effect' respectively, and they often feature in stylised models of industry dynamics; see the survey by Beath *et al.*, 1995.

7   This argument is due to Schliefer, 1986, who also introduced the distinction between 'invention' and 'implementation' used earlier.

8   See Schmookler, 1966, Stoneman, 1979, Scherer, 1982, Parker, 1992, and others. Griliches, 1990, Cohen, 1995, Scherer and Ross, 1990, and others provide useful surveys of some of this literature, while Mowery and Rosenberg, 1979, is a good critical assessment of early work on the demand pull hypothesis.

9   See Geroski and Walters, 1995. Since the innovations data get close to reflecting implementation decisions, while R&D and patenting reflect activities associated with invention, this result is not inconsistent with Saint-Paul, 1993, who found no relation between R&D spending and demand. Wyatt, 1986, reworked some of Schmookler's data and found causal relations running from investment expenditures to patenting, but not the reverse. Results reported by Walsh, 1984, and Kleinknecht and Verspagen, 1990, about the causal relation

between demand and patenting or innovation are, however, slightly less clear.

10   It is worth emphasising the weakness of our data. Given the selective nature of the effects of recessions on firms and the discrete nature of many of their responses, it is possible that the volume of investment in intangibles abandoned or postponed by some firms more than dwarfs that brought forward by others. This effect may be even more marked than with investments in tangibles, contradicting the assertion in the text.

11   See, for example, Saint-Paul, 1993, and Nickell and Nicolitsas, 1995.

12   Somewhat more generally, macroeconomic volatility is unlikely to be conducive to innovative activity. Stoneman, Diederen and Toivanen, 1995, studied the adoption of robots in 16 countries over the period 1981–93, and found that while increases in GDP and GDP growth increased optimal stocks of robots, volatility of GDP growth reduced the speed of adjustment to those stocks.

13   For some formal work embodying these ideas see Milgrom and Roberts, 1990 and, for some empirical work in the same spirit, Ichniowski and Shaw, 1995.

14   There is an extensive literature on the success of new product innovations, and much of it stresses the importance of accurate information on user needs and investments in marketing to insure success; see Freeman, 1986, and others.

15   To get some sense of the difference between these innovating firms and others, we examined the behaviour of the 243 firms who brought forward either a product innovation or a process innovation. 45 per cent of them brought forward investments in R&D, 50 per cent brought forward investments in training, 33 per cent brought forward investment in marketing and 23 per cent brought forward investments in plant and machinery. Not only was this larger group of firms less likely to bring forward investment of any kind (26 per cent brought forward only a product or a process innovation), but their reliance on training and R&D was much weaker than that of the innovators.

16   For recent work, see Geroski *et al.*, 1996, and references cited therein. The problem is that firm size and market share are relatively stable over time, while most firms produce patents or major innovations only sporadically. Variables like cash flow are often much more highly correlated to measures of innovative output. R&D expenditures are much more statistically congruent with firm size, and these correlations are typically much better determined.

17   This observation is hardly a persuasive refutation of real business cycle theory for at least two reasons: exogenous productivity shocks are not necessarily the only possible driver of fluctuations in real business cycle models, and it is certainly the case that our data on innovative activity do not exhaust the universe of observable manifestations of these productivity shocks. This said, what little the data do say is not easy to reconcile with the theory. For recent expositions and surveys of this literature, see Plosser, 1989, Stadler, 1994, and others.

References

Abraham, K. and J. Haltiwanger (1995), 'Real Wages and the Business Cycle', *Journal of Economic Literature*, 33, 1215–1264.

Abraham, K. and Katz, L. (1986), 'Cyclical Unemployment: Sectoral Shifts or Aggregate Disturbances?', *Journal of Political Economy*, Vol. 94, No. 3, 507–522.

Aghion, P. and P. Howitt (1992), 'A Model of Growth through Creative Destruction', *Econometrica*, 60, 323–351.

Aghion, P. and G. Saint-Paul (1991), 'On the Virtue of Bad Times', mimeo, EBRD, London.

Aghion, P. and G. Saint-Paul (1993), 'Uncovering Some Causal Relationships Between Productivity Growth and the Structure of Economic Fluctuations', mimeo, DELTA.

Arrow, K. (1963), 'Economic Welfare and the Allocation of Resources for Innovations', in Nelson, R. (ed), *The Rate and Direction of Innovative Activity*, Princeton University Press, Princeton.

Baden-Fuller, C. and J. Stopford (1992, *Rejuvenating the Mature Business*, Routledge, London.

Bailey, E. (1986), 'Price and Productivity Changes Following Deregulation: The US Experience', *Economic Journal*, 96, 1–17.

Barro, R. and X. Sala-i-Martin (1995a), 'Convergence across States and Regions', *Brookings Papers on Economic Activity*, Vol. 1, 107–182.

Barro, R. and X. Sala-i-Martin (1995b), *Economic Growth*, McGraw Hill, New York.

Bean, C. (1990), 'Endogenous Growth and the Pro-cyclical Behavior of Productivity', *European Economic Review*, 34, 355–363.

Beath, J., Y. Katsoulacos and D. Ulph (1995), 'Game-Theoretic Approaches to the Modelling of Technological Change', in Stoneman, P. (ed), *Handbook of the Economics of Innovation and Technological Change*, Basil Blackwell, Oxford.

Bernanke, B. and M. Parkinson (1991), 'Procyclical Labour Productivity and Competing Theories of the Business Cycle', *Journal of Political Economy*, 99, 439–459.

184   Coping with recession

Bertola, G. and R. Caballero (1990), 'Kinked Adjustment Costs and Aggregate Dynamics', in O. Blanchard and S. Fisher (eds.), *NBER Macroeconomics Annual*, MIT Press, Cambridge, Mass.

Besanko, D., D. Danove and M. Shanley (1996), *Economics of Strategy*, J. Wiley, New York.

Bhagat, S., A. Schleifer and R. Vishney (1990), 'Hostile Takeovers in the 1980's: The Return to Corporate Specialization', *Brookings Papers on Economic Activity*, 1–73.

Bhaskor, V., S. Machin and G. Reid (1993), 'Price and Quantity Adjustment over the Business Cycle: Evidence from Survey Data', *Oxford Economic Papers*, 45, 257–268.

Biggadike, E. (1976), *Entry, Strategy and Performance*, Division of Research, Graduate School of Business Administration, Harvard University.

Bird, D., M. Beatson and S. Butcher (1993), 'Membership of Trade Unions', *Employment Gazette*, May 1993, 189–196.

Bishop, M. and J. Kay (1993), *European Mergers and Merger Policy*, Oxford University Press, Oxford.

Blackburn, K. and M. Ravin (1992), 'Business Cycles in the UK: Facts and Fictions', *Economica*, 59, 383–402.

Blanchard, O. and S. Fischer (1989), *Lectures on Macroeconomics*, MIT Press, Cambridge, MA.

Blanchard, O. and L. Katz (1992), 'Regional Evolutions', *Brookings Papers on Economic Activity*, No. 1, 1–75.

Blanchflower, D. and S. Burgess (1993), 'Job Creation and Job Destruction in the UK: 1980–1990', mimeo, Centre for Economic Performance, London School of Economics.

Blanchflower, D., N. Millward and A. Oswald (1991), 'Unionism and Employment Behaviour', *Economic Journal*, Vol. 101, 815–834.

Bresnahan, T. and D. Raff (1991), 'Intra-industry Heterogeneity and the Great Depression: The American Motor Vehicles Industry, 1929–1935', *Journal of Economic History*, 51, 317–31.

Bresnahan, T. and V. Ramey (1994), 'Output Fluctuations at the Plant Level', *Quarterly Journal of Economics*, 109, 593–624.

Bronars, S. and D. Deere (1993), 'Union Organising Activity, Firm Growth and the Business Cycle', *American Economic Review*, 83, 203–220.

Buiter, W. and M. Miller (1983), 'Changing the Rules: Economic Consequences of the Thatcher Regime', *Brookings Papers on Economic Activity*, 2, 305–379.

Bunck, D. and R. Smiley (1992), 'Who Deters Entry?', *Review of Economics and Statistics*, 74, 509–521.

Burnside, C., M. Eichenbaum and S. Rebelo (1993), 'Labour Hoarding and the Business Cycle', *Journal of Political Economy*, 101, 245–273.

Caballero, R. and E. Engel (1993), 'Microeconomic Adjustment Hazards and Aggregate Dynamics', *Quarterly Journal of Economics*, 108, 359–83.

Caballero, R. E. Engel and J. Haltiwanger (1995), 'Plant Level Adjustment and Aggregate Investment Dynamics', *Brookings Papers on Economic Activity*, 1–54.

Caballero, R. and M. Hammour (1994), 'The Cleansing Effects of Recessions', *American Economic Review*, 84, 1350–68.

Campbell, J. and N. Mankiw (1987), 'Are Output Fluctuations Transitory?', *Quarterly Journal of Economics*, 102, 857–880.

Carruth, A. and R. Disney (1988), 'Where have Two Million Trade Union Members Gone?', *Economica*, 55, 1–19.

Carruth, A. and A. Oswald (1989), *Pay Determination and Industrial Prosperity*, Clarendon Press, Oxford.

Channon. D. (1973), *The Strategy and Structure of British Enterprise*, Macmillan, London.

Clark, J., C. Freeman and L. Soete (1981), 'Long Waves and Technological Developments in the 20th Century', *Futures*, August, 308–22.

Clark, K., D. Leslie and E. Symons (1994), 'The Costs of Recession', *Economic Journal*, 104, 20–36.

Claydon, T. (1989), 'Union Derecognition in Britain in the 1980s', *British Journal of Industrial Relations*, 27, 217–224.

Cochrane, J. (1988), 'How Big is the Random Walk in GNP?', *Journal of Political Economy*, 96, 893–920.

Cohen, W. (1995), 'Empirical Studies of Innovative Activity', in Stoneman, P. (ed), *Handbook of the Economics of Innovation and Technological Change*, Basil Blackwell, Oxford.

Cooper, R. and J. Haltiwanger (1990), 'Inventories and the Propagation of Sectoral Shocks, *American Economic Review*, 80, 170–190.

Cooper, R. and J. Haltiwanger (1992), 'Macroeconomic Implications of Production Bunching', *Journal of Monetary Economics*, 30, 107–127.

Cooper, R. and J. Haltiwanger (1993), 'The Aggregate Implications of Machine Replacement: Theory and Evidence', *American Economic Review*, 83, 360–382.

Crafts, N. (1992), 'Productivity Growth Reconsidered', *Economic Policy*, 15, 387–426.

Cubbin, J. and D. Leech (1983), 'The Effect of Shareholding Dispersion on the Degree of Control in British Companies', *Economic Journal*, 93, 351–69.

Cubbin, J. and S. Domberger (1988), 'Advertising and Post-Entry Oligopoly Behavior', *Journal of Industrial Economics*, 37, 123–140.

Currie, D. and A. Sentance (1994), 'An End to Boom and Bust – Can the Chancellor Deliver?', *Economic Outlook*, 18, 20–23.

Davis, S. and J. Haltiwanger (1990), 'Gross Job Creation and Destruction: Microeconomic Evidence and Macroeconomic Implications', *NBER Macroeco-*

nomics Annual, 5, 123–168

Davis, S. and J. Haltiwanger (1992), 'Gross Job Creation, Gross Job Destruction and Employment Reallocation', *Quarterly Journal of Economic*, 107, 818–63.

Davis, S., J. Haltiwanger and S. Schuh (1996), *Job Creation and Destruction*, MIT Press, Cambridge, MA.

Dickerson, A. (1994), 'The Cyclicality of British Strike Frequency', *Oxford Bulletin of Economics and Statistics*, 56, 285–303.

Disney, R., A. Gosling and S. Machin (1993), 'British Unions in Decline: What has happened to Trade Union Recognition in British Establishments?', mimeo, Centre for Economic Performance, London School of Economics.

Disney, R. (1990), 'Explanations of the Decline in Trade Union Density in Britain.' *British Journal of Industrial Relations*, 28, 2, 165–177.

Domberger, S. (1987), 'Relative Price Variability and Inflation: A Disaggregated Analysis', *Journal of Political Economy*, 95, 547–66.

Domowitz, I., G. Hubbard and B. Petersen (1986), 'Business Cycles and the Relationship between Concentration and Price-cost Margins', *Rand Journal of Economics*, 17, 1–17.

Dosi, G. (1988), 'Sources, Procedures and Microeconomic Effects of Innovation', *Journal of Economic Literature*, 26, 1120–71.

Dunne, P. and A Hughes (1994), 'Age, Size, Growth and Survival: UK Companies in the 1980's', *Journal of Industrial Economics*, 42, 115–140.

Edwards, J., J. Kay and C. Mayer (1987), *The Economic Analysis of Accounting Profitability*, Oxford University Press, Oxford.

Erickson, W. (1976), 'Price Fixing Conspiracies: Their Long Term Impact', *Journal of Industrial Economics*, 26, 189–202.

Evans, P. and B. McCormick (1994), 'The New Pattern of Regional Unemployment: Causes and Policy Significance', *Economic Journal*, May, 633–647.

Fay, J. and J. Medoff (1985), 'Labour and Output Over the Business Cycle', *American Economic Review*, 75, 638–655.

Feinstein, C. and R. Matthews (1990), 'The Growth of Output and Productivity in the UK: the 1980's as a Phase of the Post-War Period', *National Institute Economic Review*, 133, 78–90.

Fischer, S. (1981), 'Relative Shocks, Relative Price Variability and Inflation', *Brookings Papers on Economic Activity*, 2, 381–441.

Fisher, F. (1987), 'On the Misuse of the Profits-Sales Ratio to Infer Monopoly Power', *Rand Journal of Economics*, 18, 384–396.

Fisher, F. and J. McGowan (1983), 'On the Misuse of Accounting Rates of Return to Infer Monopoly Profits', *American Economic Review*, 73, 82–97.

Freeman, C. (1986), *The Economics of Industrial Innovation*, 2nd ed, MIT Press, Cambridge, MA.

Freeman, C., J. Clark and L. Soete (1982), *Unemployment and Technological Inno-*

vation, Frances Pinter, London.

Gallie, D., R. Penn and M. Rose (eds), (1996), *Trade Unionism in Recession*, Oxford University Press, Oxford.

Geroski, P. (1991), *Market Dynamics and Entry*, Basil Blackwell, Oxford.

Geroski, P. (1992), 'Price Dynamics in UK Manufacturing: A Microeconomic View', *Economica*, 59, 403–420.

Geroski, P and P. Gregg (1993), 'Coping with the Recession', *National Institute Economic Review*, 146, 64–75.

Geroski, P. and P. Gregg (1996), 'What Makes Firms Vulnerable to Recessions?', *European Economic Review*, 40, 551–558.

Geroski, P., P. Gregg and T. Desjonquieres (1995), 'Did the Retreat of UK Trade Unionism Accelerate during the 1990–93 Recession?', *British Journal of Industrial Relations*, 33, 35–54.

Geroski, P. and S. Hall (1995), 'Price and Quantity Responses to Cost and Demand Shocks', *Oxford Bulletin of Economics and Statistics*, 57, 185–204.

Geroski, P. and A. Jacquemin (1988), 'The Persistence of Profits: A European Comparison', *Economic Journal*, 98, 375–390.

Geroski, P., S. Machin and C. Walters (1995), 'Corporate Growth and Profitability', forthcoming, *Journal of Industrial Economics*.

Geroski, P. and S. Toker (1994), 'The Turnover of Market Leaders in UK Manufacturing Industry', forthcoming, *International Journal of Industrial Organization*.

Geroski, P. J. Van Reenen and C. Walters (1996), 'Innovation, Patents and Cash Flow', mimeo, London Business School.

Geroski, P. and C. Walters (1995), 'Innovative Activity over the Business Cycle', *Economic Journal*, 105, 916–28.

Gertler, M. and S. Gilchrist (1994), 'Monetary Policy, Business Cycles and the Behavior of Small Manufacturing Firms', *Quarterly Journal of Economics*, 109, 309–340.

Gomulka, J. and N. Stern (1990), 'The Employment of Married Women in the United Kingdom 1970–83', *Economica*, 57, 171–200.

Gould, M. and A. Campbell (1987), *Strategies and Styles*, Basil Blackwell, Oxford.

Gregg, P. and S. Machin (1992), 'Unions, the Demise of the Closed Shop and Wage Growth in the 1980s', *Oxford Bulletin of Economics and Statistics*, 54, 53–72.

Gregg, P., S. Machin and D. Metcalf (1993), 'Signals and Cycles: Productivity Growth and Changes in Union Status in British Companies, 1984–89', *Economic Journal*, 103, 894–907.

Gregg, P. and A. Yates (1991), 'Changes in Wage Setting Arrangements and Trade Union Presence in the 1980s', *British Journal of Industrial Relations*, 29, 361–376.

Gregg, P. and D. Wilkinson (1992), 'A Regional Model of Unemployment: Technical Report to Employment Service', mimeo, National Insitute of Economic and Social Research.

Griliches, Z. (1990), 'Patent Statistics as Economic Indicators: A Survey', *Journal of Economic Literature*, 28, 1661–1707.

Grossman, G. and E. Helpman (1991), *Innovation and Growth in the Global Economy*, MIT Press, Cambridge, Mass.

Hall, R. (1986), 'Market Structure and Macroeconomic Fluctuations', *Brookings Papers on Economic Activity*, 285–322.

Hall, R. (1991a), 'Labour Demand, Labour Supply and Employment Volatility', in O. Blanchard and S. Fisher (eds.), *NBER Macroeconomics Annual*, MIT Press, Cambridge Mass.

Hall, R. (1991b), *Booms and Recessions in a Noisy Economy*, Yale University Press, New Haven.

Harrison, A. and M. Stewart (1989), 'Cyclical Fluctuations in Strike Durations', *American Economic Review*, 79, 827–841.

Harrison, A. and M. Stewart (1994), 'Is Strike Behavior Cyclical?', *Journal of Labour Economics*, 12, 524–553.

Hart, P. and N. Oulton (1995), 'Growth and Size of Firms', mimeo, NIESR.

Hay, D. and D. Morris (1991), *Industrial Economics and Organization*, 2nd ed, Oxford University Press, Oxford.

Hay, M. and K. Kamshad (1994), 'Small Firm Growth: Intentions, Implementation and Impediments', *Business Strategy Review*, 5, 49–68.

Holt, C. (1970), 'Job Search, Phillips Wage Relation and Union Influence: Theory and Evidence', in Phelps, E. et al., *Microeconomic Foundations of Employment and Inflation Theory*, Norton.

Ichniowski, C. and K. Shaw (1995), 'Old Dogs and New Tricks: Determinants of the Adoption of Productivity-Enhancing Work Practices', *Brookings Papers on Economic Activity*, 1–66.

Kay, J. (1993), *Foundations of Corporate Success*, Oxford University Press, oxford.

Kelly, J. (1987), 'Trade Unions Trough the Recession 1980–84£', *British Journal of Industrial Relations*, 25, 275–282.

Kleinknecht, A. (1987), *Innovation Patterns in Crisis and Prosperity*, Macmillans, London.

Kleinknecht, A., E. Mandel and I. Wallerstein (1992), *New Findings in Long-Wave Research*, Macmillan, London.

Kleinknecht, A. and B. Verspagen (1990), 'Demand and Innovation: Schmookler re-examined', *Research Policy*, 19, 387–94.

Knight, K. (1987), *Unemployment: An Economic Analysis*, Croom Helm, London.

Lane, S. and M. Schary (1993), 'Business Conditions, Age of Firms and Business Failures', mimeo, Boston University.

Layard, R., S. Nickell and R. Jackman (1991), *Unemployment*, Oxford University Press, Oxford.

Lichtenberg, F. (1992a), *Corporate Takeovers and Productivity*, MIT Press, Cambridge MA.

Lichtenberg, F. (1992b), 'Industrial De-diversification and its consequences for Productivity', *Journal of Economic Behavior and Organization*, 18, 427–438.

Lilien, D. (1982), 'Sectoral Shifts and Cyclical Unemployment', *Journal of Political Economy*, Vol. 90, 777–93.

Lucas, R. (1987), *Models of Business Cycles*, Basil Blackwell, Oxford.

Machin, S. and S. Wadhwani (1991), 'The Effects of Unions on Organisational Change and Employment', *Economic Journal*, 101, 835–854.

Markides, C. (1995), *Diversification, Refocusing and Economic Performance*, MIT Press, Cambridge, MA.

Mascarenhas, B. and D. Aaker (1989), 'Strategy over the Business Cycle', *Strategic Management Review*, 10, 199–210.

Mason, R. and P. Bain (1993), 'The Determinants of Trade Union Membership in Britain', *Industrial and Labor Relations Review*, 46, 2, 332–351.

Mensch, G. (1979), *Stalemate in Technology*, Balinger, New York.

Metcalf, D. (1989), 'Water Notes Dry Up', *British Journal of Industrial Relations*, 27, 1–31.

Metcalf, D. (1990), 'Can Unions Survive in the Private Sector?' in Philpot J. (ed), *Trade Unions and the Economy: Into the 1990s*, Employment Institute: London.

Metcalf, D. (1994), 'Transformation of British Industrial Relations? Institutions, Processes and Outcomes 1980–90' in Barrell, R. (ed), *Is the British Labour Market Different?*, CUP Cambridge.

Meyer, B. (1995), 'Natural and Quasi-Experiments in Economics', *Journal of Business and Economic Statistics*, 13, 151–161.

Milgrom, P. and J. Roberts (1990), 'The Economics of Modern Manufacturing: Technology, Strategy and Organization', *American Economic Review*, 80, 511-28.

Milgrom, P. and J. Roberts (1992), *Economics, Organization and Management*, Prentice Hall, Englewood, Cliffs.

Millward, N., M. Stevens, D. Smart and W. Hawes (1993), *Workplace Industrial Relations in Transition*, Dartmouth, Aldershot.

Mowery, D. and N. Rosenberg (1979), 'The Influence of Demand on Innovation', *Research Policy*, 20, 171–8.

Mowery, D. and N. Rosenberg (1987), *Technology and the Pursuit of Economic Growth*, Cambridge University Press, Cambridge.

Muellbauer, J. and A. Murphy (1993), 'Income Expectations, Wealth and Demograghy in the Aggregate UK Consumption Function', mimeo, Nuffield College, Oxford.

Mueller, D. (1986), *Profits in the Long Run*, Cambridge University Press, Cambridge.

Mueller, D. (1990), *The Dynamics of Company Profits*, Cambridge University Press, Cambridge.

Murphy, K. and J. Zimmerman (1993), 'Financial Performance Surrounding CEO

190   Coping with recession

Takeover', *Journal of Accounting and Economics*, 16, 273–315.

Neumann, G. and R. Topel (1991), 'Employment Risk, Diversification and Unemployment', *Quaterly Journal of Economics*, 56, 1341–1366.

Nickell, S. and D. Nicolitsas (1995), 'Does Doing Badly Encourage Management Innovation?', mimeo, Insitute of Economics and Statistics, University of Oxford.

Nickell, S. (1995), *The Performance of Companies*, Basil Blackwell, Oxford.

Nickell, S., S. Wadhwani and M. Wall (1992), 'Productivity Growth in UK Companies 1975–1986', *European Economic Review*, 36, 1055–1091.

Oulton, N. (1989), 'Plant Closures and the Productivity Miracle in Manufacturing', *National Institute Economic Review*, 140, 53–59.

Parker, S. (1992), 'Industrial Invention: A Supply and Demand Model for the UK: 1961–1989', *Applied Economics*, 24, 733–38.

Penrose, E. (1959), *The Theory of the Growth of the Firm*, Basil Blackwell, Oxford.

Pissarides, C. and J. Wadsworth (1989), 'Unemployment and the Inter-regional Mobility of Labour', *Economic Journal*, Vol. 99, 739–755.

Plosser, C. (1989), 'Understanding Business Cycles', *Journal of Economic Perspectives*, 3, 51–77.

Porter, M. (1980), *Competitive Strategy*, Free Press, New York.

Prais, S. (1976), *The Evolution of Giant Firms in Britain*, Cambridge University Press, Cambridge.

Pralahad, C. and G. Hamel (1990), 'The Core Competence of the Corporation', *Harvard Business Review*, 79–91.

Quah, D. (1993), 'Empirical cross-section dynamics in economic growth', *European Economic Review*, 37, 426–434.

Quah, D. (1994), 'Convergence Empirics Across Economies with (some), Capital Mobility', mimeo, London School of Economics.

Rosenberg, N. (1974), 'Science, Invention and Economic Growth', *Economic Journal*, 84, 90–108.

Rosenberg, N. and C. Frischtak (1984), 'Technological Innovation and Long Waves', *Cambridge Journal of Economics*, 8, 7–24.

Saint-Paul, G. (1993), 'Productivity Growth and the Structure of the Business Cycle', *European Economic Review*, 37, 861–883.

Sargent, J. (1991), 'Deregulation, Debt and Downturn in the UK Economy', *National Institute Economic Review*, 137, 75–88.

Scherer, F.M. (1982), 'Demand-pull and Technological Innovation', *Journal of Industrial Economics*, 30, 225–37.

Scherer, F.M. (1992), 'Schumpeter and Plausible Capitalism', *Journal of Economic Literature*, 30, 1416–33.

Scherer, F.M. and T. Ross (1990), *Industrial Market Structure and Economic Performance*, 3rd ed, Houghton Mifflin, Boston.

Schleifer, A. (1986), 'Implementation Cycles', *Journal of Political Economy*, 94, 1163–

1190.

Schmitt, J. and J. Wadsworth (1994), 'Why are 2 million men inactive? The decline in male labour force participation rates in Britain', mimeo, Centre for Economic Performance, London School of Economics.

Schmookler, J. (1966), *Innovation and Economic Growth*, Harvard University Press, Cambridge, MA.

Segerstrom, P. (1991), 'Innovation, Imitation and Economic Growth', *Journal of Political Economy*, 99, 807–827.

Segerstrom, P., T. Anant and E. Dinopoulos (1990), 'A Schumpeterian Model of the Product Life Cycle', *American Economic Review*, 80, 1077–91.

Sentance, A. (1992), 'Rebalancing the British Economy', *The Business Economist*, 24, 22–32.

Singh, S., M. Utton and M. Waterson (1991), 'Entry Deterring Strategies by Established Firms', mimeo, University of Reading.

Sisson, K. and W. Brown (1983), Industrial Relations in the Private Sector; Donovan Revisited' in Bain, G. (ed), *Industrial Relations in Britain*, Basil Blackwell, Oxford

Smiley. R. (1988), 'Empirical Evidence on Strategic Entry Deterrence', *International Journal of Industrial Organization*, 6, 167–180.

Solomou, S. (1987), *Phases of Economic Growth, 1850–1973: Kondratieff Waves and Kuznets Swings*, Cambridge University Press, Cambridge.

Stadler, G. (1994), 'Real Business Cycles', *Journal of Economic Literature*, 32, 1750–83.

Steer, P. and J. Cable (1978), 'Internal Organization and Profit: An Empirical Analysis of Large UK Companies', *Journal of Industrial Economics*, 27, 13–30.

Stewart, M. (1991), 'Union Wage Differentials in the Face of Changes in the Economic and Legal Framework', *Economica*, 58, 155–172.

Stewart, M. (1992), 'Do Changes in Collective Bargaining Arrangements imply Declining Union Wage Differentials into the 1990s?', mimeo, University of Warwick.

Stoneman, P. (1979), 'Patenting Activity: A Re-evaluation of the Influence of Demand Pressures', *Journal of Industrial Economics*, 27, 385–401.

Stoneman, P., P. Diederen and O. Toivanen (1995), 'Macroeconomic Volatility and the Diffusion of New Technology', mimeo, Warwick Business School.

Sutton, J. (1991), *Sunk Costs and Market Structure*, MIT Press, Cambridge, MA.

Tirole, J. (1988), *The Theory of Industrial Organization*, MIT Press, Cambridge, MA.

Topel, R. (1986), 'Local Labour Markets', *Journal of Political Economy*, 94, 111–143.

Tylecote, A. (1991), *The Long Wave in the World Economy*, Routledge, London.

Vickers, J. and G. Yarrow (1988), *Privatization: An Economic Analysis*, MIT Press, Cambridge Mass.

Wadsworth, J. (1994), 'The making of the British underclass? Aggregate demand and labour force anticipation', mimeo, Centre for Economic Performance, London School of Economics.

Walsh, V. (1984), 'Invention and Innovation in the Chemical Industry', *Research Policy*, 13, 211–34.

West, M., T. Pillinger, M. Moore and S. MacPherson (1995), 'Managerial Practices, R&D and Innovation', mimeo, Institute of Work Psychology, University of Sheffield.

Whittington, R. (1991), 'Recession Strategies and Top Management Change', *Journal of General Management*, 16, 11–28.

Wilkinson, D. (1992), 'Has the North-South Divide Come to an End?' *National Institute Economic review*, 149, 88–98.

Wyatt, G. (1986), *The Economics of Invention*, Wheatsheaf Books, Brighton.

Yip, G. (1982), *Barriers to Entry: A Corporate Strategy Perspective*, lexington Books, Lexington, Mass.

Index

THE NATIONAL INSTITUTE OF
ECONOMIC AND SOCIAL RESEARCH
PUBLICATIONS IN PRINT

published by
THE CAMBRIDGE UNIVERSITY PRESS
(available from booksellers, or in case of difficulty from the publishers)

Printed in the United States
By Bookmasters